STRONG MEN SERIES STUDY

# THE DESCENT

## BOOK 4: LEADING COURAGEOUSLY

# JIM RAMOS

# COPYRIGHT

© 2021 Jim Ramos

All rights reserved. No part of this publication may be reproduced, distributed, or transmitted in any form or by any means, including photocopying, recording, or other electronic or mechanical methods, without the prior written permission of the publisher, except in the case of brief quotations embodied in critical reviews and certain other noncommercial uses permitted by copyright law. For permission requests, contact Five Stones Press or Jim Ramos

Publisher: Five Stones Press, Dallas, Texas

For quantity sales, textbooks, and orders by trade bookstores or wholesalers contact Five Stones Press at connect@fivestonespeople.com

Five Stones Press is owned and operated by Five Stones Church, a nonprofit 501c3 religious organization. Press name and logo are trademarked. Contact publisher for use.

Jim Ramos's website is www.meninthearena.org - Men in the Arena can bring speakers to your organization to teach the principles covered in this book.

All chapter entries are listed in order according to where they appear in Scripture. Unless noted the entries are from the New American Standard Bible (NASB).

All other Scripture quotations are taken from the New American Standard Bible, ©1960, 1962, 1963, 1968, 1971, 1972, 1973, 1975, 1977, 1995 by The Lockman Foundation. Used by permission. Additional versions used are:
KJV—King James Version. Authorized King James Version.
NIV—Scripture taken from the Holy Bible, New International Version®. Copyright © 1973, 1978, 1984 by International Bible Society. Used by permission of Zondervan Publishing House. All rights reserved.

Printed in the United States of America

# DEDICATION

Years ago my paid youth staff (along with a few others) thought it would be funny to rearrange the keys on my keyboard. After several attempts to type a sentence, to my chagrin not one word was spelled correctly. Disturbed by an underlined red computer screen, I stepped out of my office and asked for help. When I shared my dilemma—that something is seriously wrong with me—the office staff erupted hysterically. It was the first time I'd ever heard the term "home row."

To this day I still use the hunt-and-peck method of typing. This, combined with my uncanny ability to pass over the details, makes the Editing Team invaluable. All of our books are self-published. Men in the Arena has paid no editors or proofreaders, only these faithful volunteers. I am so blessed to have them. They have prevented some major damage! Trust me!

The Descent is dedicated to the faithful people on our Editing Team. The group of talented and incredibly patient individuals has been a saving grace. This book is dedicated to you and the many hours spent slaving over my poor typing and grammatical errors.
Thank you!

# TEAM CAPTAIN RESOURCES

You've received The Strong Men Series at a conference, from our website, your pastor, or possibly a friend. Now what? If you're holding this book, then you are a magnum enough man to figure it out on your own. This book is dangerous and has the power to change lives because within its pages are reference after reference from the Book of books.

You may still have some questions; we know this. We've provided several resources to help you on your journey to transform the lives of men and those they love, because when a man gets it—everyone wins.

First, check out our website (www.meninthearena.org). There you will find tons of great resources designed to inspire and equip you towards your best version.

Second, join thousands of men from around the world on our exciting Men in the Arena closed Facebook forum for men. Engage with men every day as they dialogue about what a man is and does. Do you need more help? We have a team of Arena Coaches ready to help you!

Third, subscribe to our wildly popular Men in the Arena Podcast. The Men in the Arena Podcast targets men living in the "Stress Bubble of Life" who are hardworking, loving one wife, raising godly children, and serving in their community.

Fourth, check out the QR Code before each meeting that links to an introductory video. Each video will help guide you to the best meeting possible.

# SEND US A PICTURE OF YOUR TEAM

## SEND US A PICTURE OF YOUR TEAM AND YOUR HERO STORY

We have no way of knowing who our resources are impacting, but we'd love to celebrate with you. Send us a picture of your team. We'll post it on social media and in our monthly newsletter if the photo is high quality and we have space.

Also, send us your stories of transformation that we call Hero Stories. God is the famous one, but He has chosen you to be the hero for your family. When a man gets it—everyone wins. If we happen to share your story, we will shoot you some swag to say, "Thanks!"

When you send the team picture, let us know where you're from (city, state, and/or country), who the leaders are, and where you meet (coffee shop, living room, church, etc.). Thank you for partnering with us.

# INTRODUCTION

*As they were coming down the mountain, Jesus instructed them, "Don't tell anyone what you have seen, until the Son of Man has been raised from the dead."*
~ Matthew 17:9

Though pain and resistance characterize the climb, most problems occur on the descent. Climbing Mt. Everest, for example, is incredibly dangerous. But most deaths occur on the descent, in the so-called "Death Zone" just above 8,000 meters.

As a young man carrying eighty pounds out of the mountains, I struggled to maintain footing on the descent. An avid backpacker, my cousin "Big" Darby instructed, "Jimmy, nose over toes. Always keep your nose over your toes."

To this day I teach people that the art of descending safely is as simple as keeping your nose over toes. The temptation, however, is to relax and lean back, which is more comfortable but dangerous. To lean over the toes when descending can be frightening, but it's where you'll find the best traction.

Nose over toes. Nose over toes.

Protecting integrity, fighting apathy, and pursuing God passionately sets the stage for men to reclaim their identities. The man who possesses the former three without taking the initiative to lead, however, is worse than losing it in the death zone. How many churches are filled with men who love the Lord, but refuse to lead; deferring leadership to the pastoral team, anonymous Sunday school teachers, or famous podcast preachers.

Men don't defer leadership. Males do.

Men accept the awesome responsibility of leading those they love, and coaching through life's adventures. At a glance, leadership seems like no big deal, but navigating down the mountain of leadership is a matter of life and death—the life and death for those a man loves.

How many times have we seen a man fall and his family come tumbling down as well? Tragically, this happens far too often. By falling I'm not only talking about sins of commission, but omission as well. There are many routes to the trails' end and many styles of Christian leadership. The male who camps passively on the summit, indifferent to the challenges waiting those he's called to lead is less than a man. Our world is filled with the collateral damage from the sins of a passive male.

How many "successful" businessmen can you name who gained the world at the expense of relationships with those they love, before we call "Foul"? When will we stop thinking money will fix our problems or cure our unwillingness to lead?

We need to redefine success. Money has nothing to do with it. If anything, the more wealth a man has the steeper the descent. Wealth adds more obstacles for a man to negotiate as he leads.

Listen carefully to wisdom. The ability to accumulate wealth is mutually exclusive from the ability to be a spiritual leader. Stop confusing them as synonymous. Oh, but money is so alluring isn't it?

It's a slippery slope when a man leans back and defers comfort over leading his family. We must overcome that temptation to lean back and relax. Instead, lean into the path you are called. Navigate down the mountain with the utmost care.

Lean into your God-given mandate to lead. Lean into your family.

Men don't defer leadership.

Nose over toes.

# TABLE OF CONTENTS

| | |
|---|---|
| *TIP OF THE SPEAR* | *10* |
| *LEAD FROM THE BACK* | *22* |
| *THE FIGHT LIST* | *32* |
| *IN MEN WE TRUST* | *44* |
| *FULL ENGAGEMENT* | *56* |
| *FATHER TO THE FATHERLESS* | *66* |
| *THE SHEPHERD* | *76* |
| *DESCENDING INTO GREATNESS* | *88* |
| *COACH OR PASTOR?* | *98* |
| *BIBLE CODES* | *108* |

# A WORD FROM THE AUTHOR

Welcome to the multimedia edition of the Strong Men Study Series. In this new edition we've added QR codes at the beginning of each chapter. You can scan the QR codes with your smartphone or tablet to access all team meeting introductory videos.

In these videos we introduce you to the content of each study. These brief presentations are designed to prepare your mind and heart for each team study.

At the end of the book you'll see a page called, "New Team Launch Steps" with QR codes leading up to your Men in the Arena team launch. The videos are a great resource for any man desiring to launch a new team. We emphatically recommend that every man partner with another man, to eventually start his own team. You've got this!

There are many QR readers available for smartphones and tablets. Check your device. It may already have one installed. Thank you so much for championing the cause of Christ on behalf of men because when a man gets it—everyone wins.

*~ Jim Ramos*

# TEAM MEETING ONE:
# TIP OF THE SPEAR

> *"Leaders are on the point. Out in full view, each one becomes a target, and each one must anticipate being shot at."*
> ~ Marshall Shelley

Welcome to the fourth book in The Strong Men Series—The Descent. Manhood is a journey more than a destination. We firmly believe that manhood is a choice. Males are born but men are made one day at a time. Like the tip of a spear, they're forged in the fires of life.

The Strong Men Series leads men up and over the allegorical mountain of manhood. The Descent: Leading Courageously was inspired by three decades observing Christian men defer spiritual leadership of their families to pastors, lay leaders, churches, and away from their biblical mandate.

Essentially, they leaned back, and relaxed as pastors and church programs formed their families spiritually. We believe in the local church but we believe even more that, ultimately, it's the man who will be held accountable for his family's spiritual growth.

Leadership can be tricky and no two leaders are the same. Choose the path of leadership that best suits you, but do something, anything, just lead.

Welcome to The Descent!

# TEAM MEETING AT A GLANCE

- Opening Prayer, Weekly Announcements
- Personal and Victory Stories
- Each man will share his story — one man per week until all men have shared.
- After all men have shared their personal story, allow time each week for them to share victory stories.
- Weekly Study Closing Prayer
- Closing Prayer

> *"There is no such thing as a self-made spiritual leader. A true leader influences others spiritually only because the Spirit works in and through him to a greater degree than in those he leads."*
> ~ J. Oswald Sanders

**What does leading a family look like? What do you do to lead yours?**

We all lead in different ways. The goal of The Descent is not to conform men to a particular style or philosophy of spiritual leadership. It's simply to convince men to lead.

Do something. Don't sit around discussing how many chest compressions and rescue breaths are needed when someone is lying on the floor unconscious. Just move. Do something! Spiritual leadership is similar.

Act. Move. Pick a route and start navigating those you love to life and freedom.

**What does it look like to lead spiritually?**

> *"As a leader, you're supposed to be above reproach, and what that means is you can't even give the appearance that you're going to do something wrong."*
> ~ Kevin Thomas

**What is the paradox in leadership between being the tip of the spear and leading from the back? How can you explain each?**

Leading from the back is stepping back, and seeing the big picture of the family's needs. It means getting behind the family and serving. It means sacrificing your needs for theirs. It means humbly getting under to lift, encourage, and support.

**Do you tend towards being the tip of the spear or leading from the back? Explain.**

As the tip of the spear, a man gets out in front of his family. He navigates the household through life. He sees ahead of them. He is the visionary. He takes the brunt of life's impact. He's the first point of contact.

**What is the tension between being the tip of the spear and leading from the back?**

*"After three years of research and study, it is my conclusion that effective male leadership is going the way of the dinosaur. Some people are worried about the extinction of whales, condors, snail darters, or baby seals. But let me shoot straight with you. I'm a lot more worried about the extinction of the men who know how to lead a family."*
~ Steve Farrar, Point Man

**What do the following verses teach us about being the tip of the spear?**
Philippians 3:17-20 and 2 Thessalonians 3:7-9

> *Carry each other's burdens, and in this way you will fulfill the law of Christ.*
> *If anyone thinks they are something when they are not, they deceive themselves.*
> ~ Galatians 6:2-3

**In the Pastoral Epistles we learn that the spiritual leaders must be an example. They should be an example of what?**
1 Timothy 4:11-16 and Titus 2:6-8

**How can you define and sharpen your skills as a spiritual leader? What do you need to do?**
Romans 12:3-4, 2 Timothy 2:21, and 4:4

> "The Tip of the Spear, what we used in the military to mean the cutting edge, breakthrough, or blitzkrieg. It's the initial strike to separate, surprise, and scatter the opposing force. Basically, you need to sharpen and define the tip. Each operation determines what kind of tip you need. So it's not always just the sharpest point that is right for the job."
> ~ Sean, Men in the Arena Facebook Forum.

**Living in full view as the (spiritual leader) tip of the spear is like living in a glass house. What do the following verses say about living above reproach? Are there any items from these lists that you struggle or disagree with? Why?**
1 Thessalonians 5:19-24 (KJV), 1 Timothy 3:1-3, 5:7, and Titus 1:5-9

> *Abstain from all appearance of evil.*
> ~ 1 Thessalonians 5:22 (King James Version)

"It's rather startling to observe in the Gospels that these early disciples really did not do much more than watch Jesus work for a year or two. He did not ask anyone to do or be anything he had first not demonstrated in his own life. It is well enough to tell people what we mean, but it is infinitely better to show them how to do it. People are looking for demonstration, not explanation."
~ Robert E. Coleman, The Master Plan of Evangelism

> "God doesn't want people to do what they think is best: he wants them to do what he knows is best, and no amount of reasoning and intellectualizing will discover that."
> ~ Henry T. Blackaby,
> Spiritual Leadership: Moving People on to God's Agenda

> *"It's harder to lead a family than to rule a nation."*
> ~ Chinese Proverb

**Look at 1 Timothy 3:1-2. How does setting up guardrails help a man remain above reproach? How do guardrails lead to more freedom, not more rules?**

*Here is a trustworthy saying: Whoever aspires to be an overseer desires a noble task. Now the overseer is to be above reproach…*
*~ 1 Timothy 3:1-2*

**Guardrails aren't legalistic rules we must follow. They are wise guidelines that direct and protect as we travel the road of life. Who may be able to question your lifestyle? Is there a blind turn that you are approaching too fast?**

Break into groups of three or four.

**How can we pray for your growth as the tip of the spear?**

Take a moment today and pray for each other.

# STUDY NOTES

For the next five days, read the following entries from our **The Field Guide: A Bathroom Book for Men.**

We hope they challenge and encourage you to get in the great Arena for God. See you on the Arena Floor!

# UPSIDE DOWN

*Finish your outdoor work and get your fields ready; after that, build your house.*
~ Proverbs 24:27

I once counseled a young "Christian" couple prior to marriage. They said they weren't in debt, but staring at the new diesel truck parked outside, the bride to be said, "I owe over thirty thousand on the truck, but that's not credit card debt." I quoted financial expert Dave Ramsey saying, "Sell the truck! You're too young to afford it. You don't deserve it."

Disappointed she responded, "But I like it." Her fiancé sat passive and silent. He married that truck a few months later, or should I say the payments. Romans 13:8 clearly teaches "Let no debt remain outstanding among you except the continued debt to love one another."

We live in an upside down world. We buy stuff before we have the money, becoming slaves to the lender (Proverbs 22:7). We buy new vehicles on credit that cost more than the car is worth as soon as we drive it off the lot.

Proverbs 24:27 depicts a farmer preparing his first crop. It admonishes men to finish the job, count the cost, collect the money, and then build the house. Jesus warned of the folly of building without counting the cost (Luke 14:28-31).

It's tough to live an upright life when you're upside down.

Be a finisher with your finances. Spend less than you earn.

You're a man. You set the financial pace in your home. Earn the money before you spend it. Do you think it's coincidental that the following two proverbs are together?

*"Start children off on the way they should go, and even when they are old they will not turn from it.*
*The rich rule over the poor and the borrower becomes slave to the lender"*
~ Proverbs 22:6-7

Are you upright or upside down?

# MAN IN THE ARENA

*The credit belongs to the man who is actually in the arena.*
~ Theodore Roosevelt

In Waking the Dead, author John Eldredge boldly states that, "men fear the glory." They fear being put on display. With the exceptions of giving and personal prayer, anonymity is a crutch for weak men. Men are called to lead, and leaders are visible. Anonymity is a trait of cowardice in a society that has neutered manhood

Did Jesus fear being put on display when he tore the Temple apart (John 2:13-17)? All the Disciples could do was stare in disbelief until one of them remembered an obscure verse in the Psalms that said, "Zeal for your house will consume me" (Psalm 69:9).

Our politically correct Bible translators simply label this event as the Cleansing of the Temple (NASB), Jesus Cleanses the Temple (ESV, NKJV), and Jesus Clears the Temple (NIV). A more accurate portrayal expressing the reality of the event should be Jesus Rips the Temple a New One. Jesus Goes Off. Jesus Kicks Ass and Takes Names.

Jesus doesn't want men to hide in their churches. Men are made for meaning and purpose. Men are formed to fight.

"'For I know the plans I have for you,' declares the Lord, 'plans to prosper you and not to harm you, plans to give you hope and a future'" (Jeremiah 29:11).

Men aren't made to hide under the shadows of indifference. Removing darkness takes courage, resolve, and tenacity. You'll be seen. You'll be noticed.

Hopefully, you'll be persecuted (2 Timothy 3:12). Our critics are either men who are paralyzed in fear or oppose the light.

Let our critics be the beacons that affirm we're doing what's right. Thank God for them. They are a symbol of life value for the man who, Roosevelt says, fights for "a worthy cause." Don't fear the glory. Put yourself on display so you, in turn, can put your God on display.

# THE GREATEST FEAR

*There is a glory to your life that the Enemy fears, and he is hell-bent on destroying that glory before you act on it.*
~ John Eldredge, Waking the Dead

Search deep for the answer to this question, "What is my greatest fear?" Is it heights? Is it depths? Is it discovering I have a terminal illness? Is it the thought of losing a child or loved one? Is it insignificance?

The most deadly fear for many men is much deeper and debilitating than any of these. Eldredge believes our greatest fear is the glory—we fear being put on display. Instead of stepping up, the great temptation is to step back into the crowd and blend in—anonymous.

Glory is simply bringing something into the light. It's drawing positive attention to that thing. Hack down a Douglas fir, strap it to your car, drive it home, decorate it, and this dead tree is suddenly noticeable. It's glorified.

The great fear of men is being put on display. What if I leave it all on the field and fail? Or worse, what if God answers my prayers and I succeed? Who will be out on display then?

Culture tells us glory is chauvinistic, arrogant, and conceited. But Jesus didn't fear being noticed. Peter didn't run from leading the early Church.

David didn't hide in the ranks like his brothers. Paul told the men of Philippi, "the things you have learned and received and heard and seen in me, practice these things"
(Philippians 4:9).

Our culture encourages men to cover up the glory. But this couldn't be further from the truth. Humility is not anonymity. God wants outspoken men, men who are bold about who He is in their lives as 1 Corinthians 10:31 tells us, "Whatever you do, do all for the glory of God."

Put yourself on display for the Master. Stop fearing the glory.

# ONE DEGREE

*No, the word is very near you; it is in your mouth and in your heart so you may obey it.*
~ Deuteronomy 30:14

*I have hidden your word in my heart that I might not sin against you.*
~ Psalm 119:11

I used to pick Colton up from middle school. One day, while pulling out of the parking lot, a strangely dressed middle school girl crossed in front of us. Her red plaid dress, long sleeve shirt, and uncut hair tied in a bun made her seem out of place. I realized she attended the private school next door.

Her school is attached to a church that doesn't follow the Apostle's Creed. They believe the Trinity is not biblical and only by the outward sign of speaking in tongues are you truly saved. They have strayed from the Word of God.

It's amazing how one error can change everything. One degree off on a compass and you're lost. One-hundredth of a second and a hundred-meter dash sprinter is out of medal contention. Miss by an inch and strike out. One inch short and your par is a putt for bogie. One foot off is an air ball. One verse out of context can be heresy.

At what point do we call these watered-down Bible paraphrases what they are—a paraphrase instead of the Bible? We have turned the most dangerous book in the world into little more than a comic book. The watered down Word of God is disastrous. Know the word men. Know it better than anyone in your family.

"Do your best to present yourself to God as one approved, a worker who does not need to be ashamed and who correctly handles the word of truth" (2 Timothy 2:15).

# LOSING HEART

*Therefore we do not lose heart. Though outwardly we are wasting away,*
*yet inwardly we are being renewed day by day.*
*~ 2 Corinthians 4:16*

Therefore we do not lose heart. Though outwardly we are wasting away,
yet inwardly we are being renewed day by day.
~ 2 Corinthians 4:16

After seven missed shots the elk was gone. It took five years to draw the tag, and the hunt was over that fast. We'd backpacked into Hell's Canyon, the deepest in America, and six days later hiked out defeated.

We watched as the elk jumped a downfall, paralleled the rim rock above, was over the ridge, and gone forever. When something is lost it's usually gone—forever. To recover something lost takes nothing short of a miracle.

We need a miracle to recover the lost identity of men. Along with the heart, the biblical identity of men has disappeared. Men have wandered. They're lost.

In a meeting with friend, Stu Weber, he shared, "When you win a man, you win the family. When you lose the man, you lose the family. When a man gets it, everyone wins."

Without the understanding of what a man was created for, he wanders aimlessly, compelling the wife to lead by default. Without his biblical identity intact, he anticipates the next day off, next game to watch, or hobby to indulge in. The man who's lost his way is often the guy on the couch wearing out the remote control.

The loss of identity is synonymous to a loss of heart. This is the greatest tragedy of our time. Like the elk disappearing over the rim rock, men are long gone with no clue what they've lost. We must rally for the hearts of men.

Together let's fight for the great asset of God—His men. If you win a man, everyone wins. If you lose the man, everyone loses.

# TEAM MEETING TWO: LEAD FROM THE BACK

> *"If you don't know where you're going, you'll probably end up somewhere else."*
> ~ David Campbell

What did you take away from last week's study and daily readings? What are you still processing? What challenged your current paradigm? What inspired you to grow as a man?

"Lead from the back" was Men in the Arena's original tagline. It was later replaced with, "When a man gets it everyone wins." The original tagline required constant explanation.

During that same time a political leader began using a similar phrase, creating even more confusion. To simplify our mission and eliminate confusion, "When a man gets it, everyone wins" was crafted.

This week, we took those passages and some others and categorized them into pieces fitting into the puzzle of integrity. The first is righteousness. What is righteousness?

What does it mean to lead from the back? Who have you seen leading from the back? How is it different from being the tip of the spear (see last week's meeting)?

Think about coaches, military leaders, and politicians. Are they out in front leading the charge as an example of sacrifice? Do they lead from the front? Or do they use their experience and expertise to lead from behind the front lines? They may have a history of being in the trenches but many leaders are forced to step back, often for their own protection, and the greater good of the vision.

# TEAM MEETING AT A GLANCE
- Opening Prayer, Weekly Announcements
- Personal and Victory Stories
- Each man will share his story — one man per week until all men have shared.
- After all men have shared their personal story, allow time each week for them to share victory stories.
- Weekly Study Closing Prayer
- Closing Prayer

> "A good leader remains focused. Controlling your destination is better than being controlled by it."
> ~ Jack Welch

Even the President of the United States, the Commander in Chief, often has no military experience. In fact, eleven United States Presidents (two of the last three) did not serve in the military.

**Where have you witnessed leaders leading from the back? How does leading from the back create tension with those reaching to get out in front? Where is the biblical balance? Where has leading from the front become more of a cultural than spiritual paradigm?**

To lead from the back is to lead from the bottom up. This is the polar opposite of most organizational flow charts.

**Check out what Jesus says about leading from the back. What did Jesus teach about spiritual leadership? How is this different from the leadership of males today?**
Matthew 20:25-28, 23:11-12, Mark 9:33-37, John 10:11-18, and 13:1-17

Jesus led from the top down: the top of the cross!

**What is the goal of spiritual leadership? How do we accomplish this within the context of our home? What are some Do's and Do Not's of spiritual leadership?**
Philippians 1:15-18, 2:3-8 and James 3:13-18

> *"The tip of the spear takes and absorbs the impact.*
> *It cuts a hole that makes way for the rest."*
> ~ Carl Swartz

*"Instead, whoever wants to become great among you must be your servant, and whoever wants to be first must be your slave—just as the Son of Man did not come to be served, but to serve, and to give his life as a ransom for many."*
~ Jesus

**How can you imitate Jesus' servant leadership in your home? Where can you grow in leading from the back? Where has pride crept into your spiritual leadership style?**

*"Not proud, not thinking of yourself as better than other people. Given or said in a way that shows you do not think you are better than other people. Showing that you do not think of yourself as better than other people."*
~ Definition of humble, Merriam - Webster Dictionary

**Would pride or humility best describe your leadership style? Why?**

**In Philippians 2:7 we read that Jesus, "emptied Himself, taking the form of a bondservant." How can you empty yourself? Where do you need to empty yourself of pride? How can you learn from Jesus?**

*who, although He existed in the form of God, did not regard equality with God a thing to be grasped, but emptied Himself, taking the form of a bond-servant, and being made in the likeness of men. Being found in appearance as a man, He humbled Himself by becoming obedient to the point of death, even death on a cross.*
~ Philippians 2:6-8 (New American Standard Bible)

"The Greek word for 'form', *morphe*, denotes the special form or feature of a person or thing; it is used with particular significance in the New Testament, only of Christ in Philippians 2:6-7, in the phrases 'being in the form of God,' and 'taking the form of a servant.'

*An excellent definition of the word is that of Gifford: 'morphe is therefore properly the nature or essence, not in the abstract, but as actually subsisting in the individual, and retained as long as the individual itself exists'."*
~ Vines Expository Dictionary of the New Testament

> *"Humility is not thinking less of yourself, it's thinking of yourself less."*
> ~ C. S. Lewis

Leading from the back is taking on the form of a servant. Rate yourself as a servant-leader in your home from 1-10 (one being the lowest and ten being the highest). Explain your answer.

*"Some persons are always ready to level those above them down to themselves, while they are never willing to level those below them up to their own position. But he that is under the influence of true humility will avoid both these extremes. On the one hand, he will be willing that all should rise just so far as their diligence and worth of character entitle them to; and on the other hand, he will be willing that his superiors should be known and acknowledged in their place, and have rendered to them all the honors that are their due."*
~ Jonathan Edwards

**Lead from the back. Be a servant leader. Be a sacrificial leader. Be a supporting leader. Be a leader that sees the bigger picture. Which of these is your greatest growth area? Explain.**

> *"Where a man belongs is up early and alone with God seeking vision and direction for his family."*
> ~ John Piper

Break into groups of three or four.

**What one area will you focus on as a servant leader in your home?**

Take a moment today and pray for each other.

# STUDY NOTES

_____
_____
_____
_____
_____
_____
_____
_____
_____
_____
_____
_____
_____
_____

For the next five days, read the following entries from our **The Field Guide: A Bathroom Book for Men.**

We hope they challenge and encourage you to get in the great Arena for God. See you on the Arena Floor!

# ABSENTEE DAD

*Know then in your heart that as a man disciplines his son, so the Lord your God disciplines you.*
~ Deuteronomy 8:5

I had coffee with a man who wanted to talk about getting his son more involved in our youth band. Knowing his son, I explained that he was a great kid, but lacked giftedness needed to be in the band. He needed more practice. But his dad refused to offer his son constructive criticism in fear of hurting his feelings.

I challenged him and his emotional response was, "Would you be that harsh with your boys on the football field?"
Would I?

On the field, my sons received the worst of my discipline because I wanted them to become better players. I guarantee that when I coached my sons nobody whispered dissension among the ranks. They earned their spot on the roster—my sons more than others.

We all know men who refuse to discipline their children. Their lack of discipline causes their children to become like overripe fruit—soft and rotten. Scripture speaks, "Whoever spares the rod hates their children, but the one who loves their children is careful to discipline them" (Proverbs 13:24). Biblical discipline is synonymous with love. Whatever happened to the trepidation felt in the words, "Wait until your father gets home"?

The absenteeism of fathers in America has robbed our young men of their identity. They're lost with no model of discipline to follow. They remind me of the young man I comforted who wept, "I've learned how to be a man by doing the exact opposite of all the men in my life."

Whether literally or figuratively absent, the passive dad lives like he hates his children. A real man accepts the responsibility for his children—no excuses.

# THE STRESS BUBBLE

*If a man is lazy, the rafters sag; if his hands are idle, the house leaks.*
~ Ecclesiastes 10:18

Imagine a line on a whiteboard labeled in increments from ten through one hundred years. Somewhere around the mid-twenties, a bubble grows and extends all the way until about the mid-fifties. We call this "The Stress Bubble." We enter this stress bubble when we start a family and it continues until our children leave the home.

Hopefully.

Two things can happen in the stress bubble. Some men blow up. They explode under pressure, lose it, and leave their family. Essentially, they burst their bubble. This can happen in the form of adultery, addiction, or abuse of the marriage covenant.

Other men simply deflate. Feeling helpless they stay in the bubble, but engage obsessively in a world of pornography, sports obsessions, selfish fun, or work. They're physically present, but absent on every other level. Like the house in today's passage, "the rafters sag (and) the house leaks." His family crumbles under his passivity and breaks down. The marriage unwinds and the children begin to run their own course.

His rafters sag.

A man who thrives inside of the bubble pushes through the demands of life, trusting God and for strength and direction (Proverbs 3:5-6). He leads those he loves. He stays engaged and carefully manages the hearts of his wife and children. He serves, directs, and pushes when needed.

Everything around him thrives even in the stress bubble.

# THE CAUSE

*But from the beginning of the creation God made them male and female.*
*For this cause shall a man leave his father and mother, and cleave to his wife…*
~ Mark 10:6-7 (KJV)

After a message I gave on the fall of man in the Garden of Eden, a young man sent this text, "So God made Eve for Adam because God said, 'It is not good for man to be lonely.' right?"
"Wrong."

Nowhere does it say that Adam was lonely. Genesis 2:18 says, "It is not good for the man to be alone."

Alone is not the same as lonely.

It's not good for a man to be alone because he needs a "helpmate." A good woman makes a good man better. Unless called to singleness, a man is incomplete without a woman. I believe the adage, "behind every good man is a good woman."

It's not good for a man to be alone—at least not this man. We can't ignore today's passage, "For this cause a man shall leave his father and mother."

Did you catch that? Marriage is bigger than not being alone, deeper than overcoming loneliness, and higher than his need for sex. Marriage is God's great Cause. It's a living parable between Christ and the Church (Ephesians 5:22-33).

After more than twenty years of marriage, Shanna has made me a better man. She pushes me more than I want to be pushed. She teaches me how to love better than I love. She sees what I don't see. She believes in me when I don't believe in myself. She challenges me to be better than I was and am.

If the man is the head of the household, then the woman is definitely the neck! God fulfills his great Cause of turning boys into men with women as their catalysts.

# STRAIGHT AND ARROW

*Folly delights a man who lacks judgment, but a man of understanding keeps a straight course.*
~ Proverbs 15:21

*In his heart a man plans his course, but the Lord determines his steps.*
~ Proverbs 16:9

The Great Hunt exists to "transform lives through teams of men." Our passion is to equip men to learn about manhood, lead biblically, and leave a legacy.

Most men go through these stages in life; learner (0-25), leader (25-55) and legacy leaver (55-100).

As we brainstormed the perfect brand to represent The Great Hunt we landed on the arrow fletching. The fletching is the sum of the three feathers attached on the back of an arrow. The fletching directs an arrow, creating balance and stabilization in flight.

But the broad head gets most of the attention. It possesses a razor's edge and is the first point of contact. The broad head is popular, visible, and draws first blood. The fletching is forgotten in the back.

The fletching gets no respect.

But the fletching is a catalyst. It offers balance and stability against the elements. It keeps the arrow from veering. The fletching directs from the back.

A man, like the fletching, leads from the back. A man has a perfect view of those closest to him. From the back he serves his family and supervises them; encouraging, pushing and admonishing along the way. Isaiah 30:21 says, "Whether you turn to the right or to the left, your ears will hear a voice behind you, saying, 'This is the way; walk in it.'"

God leads from the back. A man leads from the back.

# LEARNED IN THE WORD

*This is a copy of the letter King Artaxerxes had given to Ezra the priest, a teacher of the Law, a man learned in matters concerning the commands and decrees of the Lord for Israel.*
~ Ezra 7:11

One of my favorite mantras to men is, "Know the Word better than anyone in your family." When I preach out of 2 Timothy 3:16-17 the eyes of men light up. Months after this message, one man shared, "That message changed my life."

Finally, he had a target to shoot at.

Where has the American Church gone wrong? Has the Bible lost its potency? Is it somehow irrelevant? How can a man grow spiritually without studying God's Word? Men of God need the Word of God.

The Psalmist wrote, "How can a young man keep his way pure? By living according to your word. I seek you with all my heart; do not let me stray from your commands" (Psalm 119:9-10)

The man of God must know the Word of God better than anyone in his family.

*"All Scripture is God-breathed and is useful for teaching, rebuking, correcting and training in righteousness, so that the man of God may be thoroughly equipped for every good work."*
~ 2 Timothy 3:16-17

Manhood is understood through the Word. A man is equipped by the Word. The Word of God is a man's greatest asset.

Read the word daily. Study the Word diligently. Meditate on the Word often. A man, like the arrow fletching, provides direction for his family. That direction comes from the Word of God.

# TEAM MEETING THREE: THE FIGHT LIST

> *"The older I get, the less time I want to spend with the part of the human race that didn't marry me."*
> ~ Robert Brault

**What did you take away from last week's study and daily readings? What are you still processing? What challenged your current paradigm? What inspired you to grow as a man?**

This study is based on thoughts I took from my wife, Shanna. I'm not sure if that meant they are areas I need to work on, do well in, or men generally need to know. But my wife needs me to fight for her. She deeply desires the security of knowing her man wants her and is committed (at all costs) to fight for her.

**What does it mean to fight for your wife? What does fighting for her look like? Can you share a specific moment when you fought for your wife? Can you share a time you failed to do so?**

**Men are natural conquerors. We live for the fray. We long for the hill we may die on. If married, you probably remember fighting to win your wife's love. The confirmation came the day you placed the wedding ring on her hand. Then what? Did you move onto the next conquest, leaving your wife behind?**

Sadly, this happens all too often. Women need to be pursued all their life. One of the biggest complaints we hear is about men who stop fighting for their marriage.

This looks like many things: romance, a steady job, providing security, and raising children. And sometimes fighting for your wife means fighting with your wife!

# TEAM MEETING AT A GLANCE

- Opening Prayer, Weekly Announcements
- Personal and Victory Stories
- Each man will share his story — one man per week until all men have shared.
- After all men have shared their personal story, allow time each week for them to share victory stories.
- Weekly Study Closing Prayer
- Closing Prayer

> *"Fine speech. Now what do we do?" "Just be yourselves."*
> *"Where are you going? "I'm going to pick a fight."*
> *~ William Wallace Braveheart*

**In what areas do you fight for your wife regularly? What's your greatest source of conflict? What is her most common complaint about you? Share the one thing she most often expresses that you need to change.**

Turn to Ephesians 5:25-33. Today will be spent breaking down this passage. Look up the following passages that describe how Jesus fought for us. Consider what they mean in the context of fighting for our wives. If you are single, think about how you can fight for your wife even before you marry.

*Husbands, love your wives, just as Christ loved the church and gave himself up for her to make her holy, cleansing her by the washing with water through the word, and to present her to himself as a radiant church, without stain or wrinkle or any other blemish, but holy and blameless. In this same way, husbands ought to love their wives as their own bodies. He who loves his wife loves himself. After all, no one ever hated their own body, but they feed and care for their body, just as Christ does the church for we are members of his body. "For this reason a man will leave his father and mother and be united to his wife, and the two will become one flesh." This is a profound mystery—but I am talking about Christ and the church. However, each one of you also must love his wife as he loves himself, and the wife must respect her husband.*
*~ Ephesians 5:25-33*

> *"When a woman trusts that she is loved and accepted for who she is, when she trusts that she is first on her husband's list, when she knows there is no competition, most of the struggle of living together dissipates."*
> ~ Kerrie Palmer

**What does verse 25 mean, "He gave himself up for her"? What did Jesus give himself up for? Was he reciprocating a deep love that the church gave him, or was it is a love manifested through sacrifice?**
Matthew 20:28, John 3:16-17, 1 Corinthians 15:3-4, and 1 Peter 3:18

Unhealthy marriages operate like a ledger in a checkbook. We give love after it's been given to us. Or we love when we think it will be reciprocated. We keep account of each other's checks and balances. We are ledger people. But Jesus doesn't keep score. He sacrificially gave, expecting nothing in return.

**Jesus set the bar high in verse 26. Jesus' plan for the church was to make her holy by, "cleansing her by the washing with water through the word." Only through the blood of Jesus are we washed of sin—forgiven. But what does it mean to wash your wife in the word? How do we accomplish this? Why is it important in making our wives holy?**
Colossians 1:21-23 and 1 John 1:8-10

**How do we put verse 27 in the context of marriage? Our mandate as husbands is to, "present her to himself as a radiant church, without stain or wrinkle or any other blemish, but holy and blameless." How do guardrails help keep a marriage holy and blameless? How can you help your wife maintain her integrity? Does your wife have a blind spot that demands your attention? Fight for her integrity.**
Deuteronomy 22:8, Proverbs 22:5, Galatians 6:1-2, and 1 Peter 3:1-7

> *"Don't marry the person you think you can live with; marry only the individual you think you can't live without."*
> ~ James C. Dobson

**In verse 29 (see verse 28) we read that men should care for their wives like they, "feed and care for their body, just as Christ does the church." What does this mean in the context of an obese culture? Who gets more nurturing from you—your wife or your own body?**
Nahum 1:7, Matthew 6:25-34, 11:28-30, 1 Thessalonians 2:6-8, and 1 Peter 5:6-7

**In verse 31 we read, "For this reason a man will leave his father and mother and be united to his wife, and the two will become one flesh." Besides love-making, what does it look like to be fused to your wife? What are some ways to connect with her? Older men, help the younger men on this one.**
Genesis 2:23-25, John 14:15-20, and 1 Corinthians 6:19-20

*23 The man said, "This is now bone of my bones and flesh of my flesh; she shall be called 'woman,' for she was taken out of man." 24 That is why a man leaves his father and mother and is united to his wife, and they become one flesh. 25 Adam and his wife were both naked, and they felt no shame.*
*~ Genesis 2:23-25*

> *"A happy marriage is the union of two good forgivers."*
> ~ Robert Quillen

When this meeting was being crafted I asked Shanna what she thought fighting for your marriage should look like for a man. She gave me the following list. I wondered if it was meant more for me than for you!

> *"Often times fighting for your wife means fighting with your wife."*
> ~ Anonymous

**Oh, well. Here it is anyway. I hope it helps. Discuss Shanna's "Fight List" for men.**

**Fight List #1**: Fight to honor her publicly.
Happy wife. Happy life.

**Fight List #2**: Fight to protect her.
*"There is something fierce in every man. A man needs a battle to fight; he needs a place for the warrior in him to come alive and be honed, trained, seasoned…Every man has an adventure to live, battle to fight, and a beauty to rescue."*
~ John Eldredge, Wild at Heart

**Fight List #3**: Fight for the integrity of the family unit.
*"Coming together is a beginning; keeping together is progress; working together is success."*
~ Henry Ford

**Fight List #4**: Fight to earn her respect.
*Respect is the greatest gift a woman can give her husband. Be a man worthy of it…and the wife must respect her husband.*
~ Ephesians 5:32

**Fight List #5**: Fight to make her feel safe and secure.
*"Eve is a life giver; she is Adam's ally. It is to both of them that the charter for adventure is given. It will take both of them to sustain life. And they will both need to fight together."*
~ John Eldredge, Wild at Heart

**Fight List #6**: Fight to lead her spiritually.

> *"We come to love not by finding a perfect person, but by learning to see an imperfect person perfectly."*
> ~ Sam Keen

# STUDY NOTES

For the next five days, read the following entries from our **The Field Guide: A Bathroom Book for Men.**

We hope they challenge and encourage you to get in the great Arena for God. See you on the Arena Floor!

# THE BLESSING

*After Isaac finished blessing him and Jacob had scarcely left his father's presence, his brother Esau came in from hunting. He too prepared some tasty food and brought it to his father. Then he said to him, "My father, sit up and eat some of my game, so that you may give me your blessing."*
~ Genesis 27:30-31

I sat in Hume Lake's Snack Shack after Chapel with a young man. He was clearly emotional when I walked in. Through tears, he explained that he hadn't seen his dad in years. His dad never watched him play in a football game, wrestling or track-and-field event. Then, in an act of vulnerability he leaned towards me, buried his hands in his face and wept, "I just want my Dad to tell me he's proud of me."

Today we come to a tragic story known as "The Stolen Blessing" (NASB). With the help of his mother, Jacob steals the blessing as the first-born son from his twin brother, Esau. Listen to the desire for a father's blessing in Genesis 27:34: "When Esau heard his father's words, he burst out with a loud and bitter cry and said to his father, 'Bless me—me too, my father!'"

The blessing from father to a son is empowering. It's vital to the livelihood of a child. It can be devastating if withheld.

My Dad has a deep love for his children, but struggles to articulate it. Over the years I've laughed—and cried—at the expensive birthday cards that express Dad's great pride, love, and admiration for his children. It's in those cards I've received a father's blessing.

Years ago I wrote a booklet called, Tell Him. It's a list of hundreds of blessings from a father to a son such as, "Tell him you are proud of him. Tell him he's smart. Tell him he's strong. Tell him God has a wonderful plan for him. Tell him he's handsome. Tell him there is no other like him. Tell him he's gifted."

Bless your children. Bless them often. Bless them with the powerful words that only a Father can give.

# GANGRENE JESUS

*Do your best to present yourself to God as one approved, a worker who does not need to be ashamed and who correctly handles the word of truth.*
~ 2 Timothy 2:15

I once shot a beautiful four-point Blacktail buck using a muzzleloader. I named him "Mounty" in honor of what he was doing moments before I shot him. At least he died happy!

We processed the buck in freezing temperatures and the carcass was curing as planned until the weather shifted and I noticed a slight odor. Upon inspection, I discovered an area I'd missed cleaning that began to rot the meat. Fortunately, I found it in time.

In 2 Timothy 2:17 Paul mentions Hymenaeus and Philetus whose doctrine began to "spread like gangrene." From verses 14-16 it appears that their "worldly and empty chatter" revolved around the doctrines of Christ.

Paul affirms this in verse 15, "Be diligent to present yourself approved by God as a workman who does not need to be ashamed, accurately handling the word of truth" (NASB).

Know the Word of God. Are you sick of me saying this yet? Know it enough to sniff out the stench surfacing in the modern church. It's the rank smell of those who don't know the Word of God. It's the flatulent odor of men who have given up the responsibility of knowing the Word of God better than anyone in their household, to their wives and even their children!

Recognize the sweet aroma of the "word of truth" in order to sniff out the stench of deception that justifies a man not taking responsibility for the Word of God in his home (Ephesians 5:26).

# WALK THIS WAY

*Jesus answered, "Are there not twelve hours of daylight? A man who walks by day will not stumble, for he sees by this world's light. It is when he walks by night that he stumbles, for he has no light."*
~ John 11:9-10

BJ dropped me off at the top of a six-mile-long ridge and I made the hike down it in quest of the monster buck we spotted earlier that morning. I arrived at where I thought the big boy would be with only fifteen minutes of daylight remaining.

But stumbling blindly in the rain and dense fog, I accidentally kicked a large rock that alerted everything on the hillside to my presence. Across the canyon, I caught movement of six deer including the monster, cresting the ridge and gone forever.

Now, I realized I had another problem. How would I get off this vertical hillside alive? With the headlamp casting shadows through the rain, my depth perception was skewed but thankfully I made it to the truck in one piece.

In John 11:9-10 Jesus compares the man who walks in the darkness with him who walks in the light. The man who "walks by day will not stumble." The man who confesses and repents of his sin keeps it in view of others and lives with clarity and purpose.

But "when he walks by night…he stumbles, for he has no light." When he chooses to keep his darkness a secret, he carries the added burden of sin, and is less effective as a follower of Jesus and a man.

We're judged by our actions more than intentions. Actions speak louder than words. Don't walk down the steep slope of darkness alone. You'll only injure yourself and those you love. Illuminate your darkness with the light of confession and repentance.

"Therefore confess your sins to each other and pray for each other so that you may be healed. The prayer of a righteous person is powerful and effective" (James 5:16).

# JULY EYES

*Lazy hands make a man poor, but diligent hands bring wealth. He who gathers crops in summer is a wise son, but he who sleeps during harvest is a disgraceful son.*
~ Proverbs 10:4-5

Ben was one of my all-time most committed youth workers. "Farmer Ben" taught me many things about his profession. During the summer he'd disappear for two to three months, working twenty-hour days, becoming a zombie-like manifestation of the normal Ben.

One year in particular was no different. Ben began harvest and we didn't see him until mid-August at our annual river baptism held on his farm. He wore sunglasses that day, uncommon for a guy who wears sunglasses about as often as he drinks coffee—never. Jokingly, I took off his glasses and sure enough, his eyes were bloodshot from two months of sleep deprivation.

"Wow!" I exclaimed, "You have July eyes in mid-August!"

Harvest is where the rubber meets the road for a farmer. Most of the income for a year is harvested in that three-month window. A man goes through a similar season during the twenty-five years or so he raises a family, affectionately called "The Stress Bubble." His worth as a man and leader is determined during these years.

During this season a man must work to support his family, raise his children, love his wife, and find moments to renew his spirit. Often, times for personal renewal come few and far between.

During The Stress Bubble, a man might be tempted to get "lazy hands" instead of July eyes. Fatigue often tempts him to revert to the boyish behaviors of his youth instead of the assertive actions of a man.

Vince Lombardi once said, "Fatigue makes cowards of us all." Fight to maintain diligence during the seasons when fatigue desires to conquer a man.

Always remember that July eyes are better than lazy hands.

# A TIME TO FIGHT

*After I looked things over, I stood up and said to the nobles, the officials and the rest of the people, "Don't be afraid of them. Remember the Lord, who is great and awesome, and fight for your brothers, your sons and your daughters, your wives and your homes."*
~ Nehemiah 4:14

Childhood friend, Ricky Little, once bullied my little brother to tears. Trained by Dad to defend my younger siblings at all costs, Ricky saw the fury in my eyes and ran for home. But I caught him at the doorstep, punched him in the nose, and retreated home.

When Mom found out (Mom's rules were different than Dad's) she made me apologize. But when I knocked on his door, Ricky's giant Dad opened it in full deputy uniform! Why their last name was "Little" I'll never know. He frowned at me as he applied pressure to Ricky's bleeding nose.

I stuttered through my four-year-old version of an apology and the giant Mr. Little graciously accepted. I learned a great lesson that day.

The older I get, the more I see men misinterpreting Jesus' words to "turn the other cheek" in Matthew 5:39 to mean "shut up and take it."

The Old Testament, however, gives us a more masculine interpretation of God's intent regarding fighting. I believe Dad was close to the heart of God when he taught us to never fight unless it was to protect the weak. I'll gladly turn the other cheek when persecuted for my faith, but I'll fervently bloody any nose to protect the ones I love, or the defenseless.

The people were afraid. Nehemiah knew it. But Nehemiah spoke to something greater than fear. He reminded them of God's strength. He appealed to the primary love of the men—their families.

Notice that he spoke to the men. Why? Because men are the natural protectors.

# TEAM MEETING FOUR:
# IN MEN WE TRUST

> "You don't marry one person; you marry three: the person you think they are, the person they are, and the person they are going to become as a result of being married to you."
> ~ Richard Needham

**What did you take away from last week's study and daily readings? What are you still processing? What challenged your current paradigm? What inspired you to grow as a man?**

Get over the lie that your children are more important than your wife. This is crucial, especially for second and third marriages where stepchildren are involved. Telling your wife that the kids are more important than her is cruel, not biblical, and spiritually ignorant. If your children are truly important, then loving their mom (or stepmom) will be an even higher priority than loving them.

**Last week we took a long, hard look at marriage from Ephesians 5:25-33. Who will summarize this passage in a sentence? What does it meant to be Christ to your wife?**

Your wife should be the most important person on the planet. And your marriage will struggle until she believes that. What you do on a regular basis to affirm that your wife is your most important person is more important, by far, than what you tell the guys in this room.

# TEAM MEETING AT A GLANCE

- Opening Prayer, Weekly Announcements
- Personal and Victory Stories
- Each man will share his story — one man per week until all men have shared.
- After all men have shared their personal story, allow time each week for them to share victory stories.
- Weekly Study Closing Prayer
- Closing Prayer

> *"Manhood is something a man earns. One deed at a time, one task at a time, one interaction at a time."*
> ~ David Murrow

Now, let's look at Ephesians 5:22-25. Women cringe when they hear the word "submit." Pastor's cringe when they have to teach on it. But it's a simple word. Men are called to live a life of sacrifice for their wives.

**Women are called to an attitude of submission—trust in their godly husband's leadership. Where sacrifice is an action, submission is an attitude. How do you explain submission? Why is this important to God? Why is this important to the family structure?**
Ephesians 5:22-24, Colossians 3:17-19, and 1 Peter 3:1-7

> *Wives, submit yourselves to your own husbands as you do to the Lord. For the husband is the head of the wife as Christ is the head of the church, his body, of which he is the Savior. Now as the church submits to Christ, so also wives should submit to their husbands in everything.*
> ~ Ephesians 5:22-24

> *"I have learned that only two things are necessary to keep one's wife happy. First, let her think she's having her own way. And second, let her have it."*
> ~ Lyndon B. Johnson

> *"Pursue your wife. Keep her heart as your target. Women are won when men take responsibility and prepare for their date night. Refuse to let your job, hobbies, busyness, lack of money, family obligations, or anything else take its place."*
> ~ Kerrie Palmer

**A woman may struggle to trust a male, but she will trust a man. Like it or not men, even the most mature Christian woman will struggle to submit her life into the hands of an untrustworthy male. Yes, she is mandated in Scripture to submit to you, but submission can't be forced, but it can be earned. Are there any areas in your marriage where your wife struggles to submit to you because of a lack of trust?**

*'Hupotasso' is a Greek military term meaning 'to arrange (troop divisions) in a military fashion under the command of a leader.' In non-military use, it was 'a voluntary attitude of giving in, cooperating, assuming responsibility, and carrying a burden.'"*
~ Biblestudytools.com

**Submission is about order and structure. Outside of mixed martial arts, submission is a word used mostly by followers of Jesus. As the spiritual leaders we are called to create order in the home, first through our submission to Jesus Christ. What does submission to Jesus mean for you?**
Romans 10:2-4, Hebrews 12:8-10, and James 4:6-8

*"(Submission is) the divine calling of a wife to honor and affirm her husband's leadership and help carry it through according to her gifts. It's the disposition to follow a husband's authority and an inclination to yield to his leadership."*
~ John Piper

**What do you do to put your wife first? What do you do to earn her submission? If she were here now would she agree that you put her ahead of all other people—even the children? How do you target her trust?**

> *"To find someone who will love you for no reason, and to shower that person with reasons, that is the ultimate happiness."*
> ~ Robert Brault

> *"She trusts you when you keep your covenant with God and one another as your top priority. Trust is based on a relentless commitment to your covenant with God and one another. Ultimately, a man's behavior speaks the loudest to a woman. While words are important, trust will not occur until the words are backed with action."*
> ~ Kerrie Palmer

**Is it easier to be a woman called to submit to the spiritual leadership of a trustworthy man? Or, is it easier to live a sacrificial life unto Christ placing the care of his wife equal to, or higher than, his own life?**

"I've trusted you for twenty years and you've never let me down. I will trust you now." Shanna Ramos, when I proposed risking it all to launch The Men in the Arena full time.

**"Submission is an attitude that leads to an action, but sacrifice is an action that leads to an attitude." What is true about this statement? How will your sacrificial love earn her trust?**

> *"Marriage has the power to set the course of your life as a whole. If your marriage is strong, even if all the circumstances in your life around you are filled with trouble and weakness, it won't matter. You will be able to move out into the world in strength."*
> ~ Timothy Keller

Growing up, we loved to fish for halibut. We'd hook a live anchovy through the nose and drop it to the bottom of the bay. Halibut attack the bait from the tail forward, slowly inhaling it. When we'd get a strike, Dad would tell us to let it run and give it time to think it's safe. After giving it enough line, we'd set the line and hook the unsuspecting fish.

> *"The best thing a father can do for his children is to love their mother."*
> ~ John Wooden

**Let's target her trust. What tools can you put in your "Trust Toolbox"?**

**Let's go clockwise around the room and share one thing you do to target (to earn and keep) your wife's trust.**

**What other ideas can you come up with to make your wife a priority?**

**What else can you do or say that will make her feel like the most important person on the planet?**

Break into groups of three or four.

**What one thing will you start today to show your wife she's the number one person in your life?**

Take a moment today and pray for each other.

> *"Somewhere down inside the typical lady is a 'security gland' and when financial stress enters the scene, that gland will spasm. This spasmodic gland will affect your wife in ways you can't always predict."*
> ~ Dave Ramsey

# STUDY NOTES

For the next five days, read the following entries from our **The Field Guide: A Bathroom Book for Men.**

We hope they challenge and encourage you to get in the great Arena for God. See you on the Arena Floor!

# SHADOW BOXING

*Therefore I do not run like a man running aimlessly; I do not fight like a man beating the air. No, I beat my body and make it my slave so that after I have preached to others, I myself will not be disqualified for the prize.*
~ 1 Corinthians 9:26

1 Corinthians 9:24-26 is a special passage. As a high school student, and not a follower of Jesus, it's the first passage I ever read. Diligently seeking the Bible's relevance in the life of an unsaved young man, I spent countless hours searching my Bible's concordance for anything inspiring.

When I discovered this passage, I knew I had hit gold. It resonated with a young man searching for answers. It still does.

Reaching out to the men of the undisciplined Corinthian church, Paul spoke to their athleticism to illustrate the disciplines of a godly life. Note, however, that he never condemned the fighters in this congregation. At first glance it actually appears that Paul might have boxed a little himself, "Therefore I do not run like a man running aimlessly; I do not fight like a man beating the air" (26).

The Christian life is like a boxing match.

A fighter's training not only involves learning how to throw a punch but how to take a punch. Paul knew how to take punches and how to throw them. The Christian life is not one of passive observance, but assertive perseverance and discipline. Train your faith like the boxer. Train to throw the punch, and train to take it.

As the spiritual catalyst in your home what are you doing to train your wife and children? Do they have what it takes to take any punches life may throw? Can they return the favor?

What is your spiritual training teaching others?

# BLACK FRIDAY

*The sorrows of those will increase who run after other gods.*
~ Psalm 16:4

I pen this entry the day after Thanksgiving, known as Black Friday, which is one of the busiest shopping days of the year. In 2006, Americans spent 450 billion dollars on Christmas alone. This amount exceeded the 28.2 billion dollars given in foreign aid the same year. And it all happened in one day.

Think about it. We spent 450 billion dollars for a birthday that isn't even ours! On Jesus' birthday we give and receive gifts, but what does Jesus receive? I confess that for most of my life I've "run after" the god of Christmas. I still do. This troubles me. Besides becoming a Jehovah's Witness, I'm not sure what to do. That was a joke.

Ironically, Black Friday only creates "sorrows" in our already stress-filled lives. Many max out credit cards in one day, children develop an unhealthy sense of entitlement, and Jesus becomes little more than a manger scene on a living room mantle. Maybe we should be asking, "Jesus, what do you want us to give to you for your birthday?"

Give honor to those days that deserve honor, especially birthdays and rites of passage. Let Christmas be about the God of the universe who arrived in a feed trough. It's important to lead our families closer to Jesus, even if it means further from the

Christmas-tree-mentality that's so prevalent in our culture. We need to open our eyes as spiritual leaders and see the big picture of how our reckless spending is creating an unhealthy sense of entitlement in our children.

"The god of this age has blinded the minds of unbelievers, so that they cannot see the light of the gospel of the glory of Christ, who is the image of God" (2 Corinthians 4:4).

# THE PLOTTER FEATURE

*I run in the path of your commands, for you have set my heart free.*
~ Psalm 119:32

Before smartphones, I owned a GPS (Global Positioning System) that mostly stayed in my drawer. I didn't have the patience to figure it out and add another half-pound to my already heavy pack. Since I own two topographical maps of the areas I explore, it's easier to leave the heavy GPS at home.

"Big" Darby caused me to reconsider. On one trip to New Mexico, he used the "plotter" function and it saved us from what could've become a bad deal. The plotter's most important function is the ability to navigate through the darkness by following its backtracks to the point of origin.

In unknown territory, this feature is literally a lifesaver.

The Word of God is like the plotter feature on the GPS. Listen to Psalm 119:105, "Your word is a lamp to my feet and a light for my path."

The plotter feature is one's vision in the darkness. But we're designed for more than navigating out of the darkness. The plotter works when darkness covers the knowledge of the land. Expertise in the Word equips a man to run through life instead of stumbling through the darkness.

When he knows the Word of God, he's able to navigate not only for himself but those he's charged to lead, specifically his family. Men who blaze their own trail soon discover (if they're lucky) that they have wandered off course.

Man is equipped to plot his trail by following the Bible's instructions. "Trust in the Lord with all your heart and lean not on your own understanding; in all your ways acknowledge him, and he will make your paths straight" (Proverbs 3:5-6).

Know God's Word. Walk, better yet, run, with God.

# HALF TIME

*Assemble the people—men, women and children, and the aliens living in your towns—so they can listen and learn to fear the Lord your God and follow carefully all the words of this law. Their children, who do not know this law, must hear it and learn to fear the Lord your God as long as you live in the land you are crossing the Jordan to possess.*
~ Deuteronomy 31:12-13

Memories of halftime included frantic adjustments scribbled on a chalkboard, talking to individual athletes, and attempting to create a second half advantage. Halftime is when coaches put their strategy on the board and make the adjustments needed to finish strong and win the game.

Similarly, every man eventually enters the halftime of life. He begins to ask questions such as "How can I play a better second half than the first? What is my best play? What adjustments do I need to make? What are my greatest assets? How can I overcome fear to win? Who are my greatest opponents?"

Some rightly call it a mid-life crisis when the answers to these questions result in crisis choices. Success in the second half requires sticking to a winning game plan. That plan is outlined in the Bible. Know the Word of God. Teach it to your family. Know it better than anyone in your home.

Adjustments are only helpful to those willing to learn, change, and go for the win. Become a student of the Word. Leaders are learners. Men are leaders; therefore, men are learners.

The older a man gets the easier it is to get stuck in a rut. Don't be that man! Hold to the passion of your youth. Stand on the convictions that have you where you are. Be willing to make the necessary adjustments to win the second half.

# DO NOT FEAR THE GLORY

*When the Israelites saw the man, they all ran from him in great fear.*
~ 1 Samuel 17:24

In Waking the Dead, John Eldredge states that one of man's great fears is the glory. As much as men love to brag, according to Eldredge, most men fear being put on public display.

John Wesley, the founder of Methodism, once said, "I just set myself on fire and people come to watch me burn." Wesley didn't fear the glory. Glory is a fancy word for putting something on display, similar to decorating a tree at Christmas.

Once I was asked, "What if God really does answer your prayers for The Great Hunt? What if your ministry explodes?"

The question rocked me to the core. I quietly shuddered, "God would never do that!" But the more I pondered it the more my heart raced and my palms sweat. Do I really want God to answer my prayers? At the time I thought it would be much easier to fail miserably, fold up shop, and move away to some land of anonymity.

To allow the world to watch The Great Hunt change the culture of manhood is too much pressure for a man to handle—but not God. When it comes to spiritual leadership, men can't fear the glory of being on display by God.

God wants to put men on display. That means you. He wants a man to stand up for his woman, children, and church. Humbly start praying, "Lord, put me on display." He wants men to lead the way. He wants to put you on display.

When a man decides to shine for God he can stand with the great men of old and say, "May I never boast except in the cross of our Lord Jesus Christ, through which the world has been crucified to me, and I to the world" (Galatians 6:14).

Don't fear the glory. Rather, embrace it.

# TEAM MEETING FIVE: FULL ENGAGEMENT

> "Each day of our lives we make deposits in the memory banks of our children."
> ~ Charles R. Swindoll

**What did you take away from last week's study and daily readings? What are you still processing? What challenged your current paradigm? What inspired you to grow as a man?**

If Proverbs 31 is the chapter that defines women, then Job 29 is the defining chapter for men.

**What does it look like to be fully engaged with your children while they are in the home? How do you stay connected to your adult children?**
Job 1:4-5

Men have been fed wrong narrative. Our culture tells us to work grueling hours and then disengage, remote in hand, on the couch. Our children seem to get our leftovers. Jesus wasn't married but always had time for the little children. We would be wise as men called to steward our children to make time for them every day.

**How do you stay fully engaged after work? How does exhaustion play a role in a man's disengagement from his children?**

# TEAM MEETING AT A GLANCE

- Opening Prayer, Weekly Announcements
- Personal and Victory Stories
- Each man will share his story — one man per week until all men have shared.
- After all men have shared their personal story, allow time each week for them to share victory stories.
- Weekly Study Closing Prayer
- Closing Prayer

> *"It is easier to build strong children than to repair broken men."*
> ~ Frederick Douglass,
> Abolitionist and Statesman

Today we're taking a look at the life of Job; specifically, the loss of his children. Read about the tragic loss of Job's children in Job 1:18-22.

*While he was still speaking, yet another messenger came and said, "Your sons and daughters were feasting and drinking wine at the oldest brother's house, when suddenly a mighty wind swept in from the desert and struck the four corners of the house. It collapsed on them and they are dead, and I am the only one who has escaped to tell you!" At this, Job got up and tore his robe and shaved his head.*
*Then he fell to the ground in worship and said: "Naked I came from my mother's womb, and naked I will depart. The Lord gave and the Lord has taken away; may the name of the Lord be praised." In all this, Job did not sin by charging God with wrongdoing.*
*~ Job 1:18-22*

> *"To be fully engaged, we must be physically energized, emotionally connected, mentally focused, and spiritually aligned with a purpose beyond our immediate self-interest…Full engagement requires drawing on four separate but related sources of energy: physical, emotional, mental, and spiritual."*
> ~ Jim Loehr and Tony Schwartz,
> The Power of Full Engagement

Turn to Job 29:1-5 where Job reflects on the days when his children were alive. Notice that Job had no regrets about the time he didn't spend with his children. Instead, he reflected on the connection he had with them. If your children (adult or otherwise) were tragically taken from you could you say the same thing? Is there any damage you need to repair in a relationship with one of your children?

*Job continued his discourse: "How I long for the months gone by, for the days when God watched over me, when his lamp shone on my head and by his light I walked through darkness! Oh, for the days when I was in my prime, when God's intimate friendship blessed my house, when the Almighty was still with me, and my children were around me, when my path was drenched with cream and the rock poured out for me streams of olive oil.*
*Job 29:1-6*

**How do you interpret Job 29:5, "and my children were around me"? What does it mean to have your children around you? It's one thing to be in proximity to your children but it's quite another to be present.**

**How do you stay close to your kids? How do you stay fully engaged even after a long day at work?**

**In three out of the four gospel accounts Jesus rebukes his disciples for hindering the little children. What did he say? How can we translate that into daily life? In what ways do we hinder our children from coming to us as fathers?**
Matthew 19:13-14, Mark 10:13-15, and Luke 18:15-17

**In three out of the four gospel accounts Jesus rebukes his disciples for hindering the little children. What did he say? How can we translate that into daily life? In what ways do we hinder our children from coming to us as fathers?**
Matthew 19:13-14, Mark 10:13-15, and Luke 18:15-17

**What's the greatest temptation to pull away from your children? What tools do you have to fight weariness and stay fully engaged with your children? What advice can our elders offer about staying close to our adult children?**

**Do you have a plan of action for the hours of 6:00-9:00 p.m. while children are, "around me" (Job 29:5)?**

Break into groups of three or four.

Take a moment today and pray for each other.

*"Children need models rather than critics."*
~ Joseph Joubert, French Moralist

# STUDY NOTES

For the next five days, read the following entries from our **The Field Guide: A Bathroom Book for Men.**

We hope they challenge and encourage you to get in the great Arena for God. See you on the Arena Floor!

# MONUMENTS

*These stones are to be a memorial to the people of Israel forever… He did this so that all the peoples of the earth might know that the hand of the Lord is powerful and so that you might always fear the Lord your God.*
~ Joshua 4:7 and 24

I have a house rule that if something hasn't been used for a year we get rid of it. The exception, of course, is anything in my wife's closet or the antlers hanging in the garage. My antlers have been accumulating dust dating to 1978. Each, however, points to a memory and monument in my life.

We see monuments in the story of the crossing into the Promised Land as well. Joshua selected representatives from each of the twelve tribes and instructed them to build two pyramids, one in camp (Joshua 4:1-3) and one in the Jordan (Joshua 4:4-10).

These basketball-sized rocks were to be memorials to God's deliverance. The Bible records that the monument set up in the Jordan River is there to this day!

Verses 23 and 24 tell us why: "For the Lord your God dried up the Jordan before you until you had crossed over. The Lord your God did to the Jordan just what he had done to the Red Sea."

Only Joshua and Caleb experienced both crossings and it was critical that people memorialized these events so they'd always fear God. There's a wonderful take-away for us today. Establish monuments as reminders for you to fear God. Monuments of faith point to God's provision. The Bible is a monument of God's salvation.

The baby dedication letter is a monument of parenting. The wedding ring is a monument of the marriage covenant. That baptism certificate is a monument of biblical obedience. Reflect often on these monuments of faith and victory.

# THE TENDERS

*But Abel brought fat portions from some of the firstborn of his flock. The Lord looked with favor on Abel and his offering.*
~ Genesis 4:4

One of my favorite rewards of hunting is sharing hunting successes with friends. I love pulling frozen packages out of the freezer and explaining the story behind each hunt, the cut of steak, and the way I like to prepare it. As much as I love sharing, I never share the tenderloins. The "tenders" are surrounded by fat, located in the upper cavity of the animal towards the back. They are so tender. They melt in your mouth—thus, the name.

Nope, the tenders are for me.

The more tender the meat, the better the taste. The younger the animal, the more tender the meat. A big old buck has the toughest meat to eat. Dad often bragged about his little bucks, "You can't boil the horns!" And yes, we know they're actually antlers.

It's difficult to judge the taste of similar types of fruit, but not so with cuts of meat.

Fruit is fruit and a vegetable is a vegetable.

This is where today's story gets interesting. Not only did Abel raise, harvest, and butcher his flock, but probably knew each animal by name. Abel offered the best of his meat, the "firstborn of his flock," not the leftovers. From the firstborn he offered the "fat portions," most likely the tenderloins.

I can hear his father Adam saying, "Hey, I am tired of chewy round steak! Where are those loin cuts?"

"Sorry Dad, I offered them to God."

"You did what? You're grounded!"

But God accepted the best of what Abel had to offer. Give God the first and the best, and not your leftovers.

# RAISE THE BLADE

*By faith Abraham, when God tested him, offered Isaac as a sacrifice.*
~ Hebrews 11:17

When I was a new follower of Christ, I read Jesus' command to "Sell everything you have and, then come follow me" (Mark 10:21). Responding to God's Word, I gave my brother Tom all my fishing gear. I gave my comic book collection to a teen who later sold them for drugs.

I had a garage sale where I sold my beer stein, knife, fishing pole (tougher), and antique fishing reel collections. I was left with my truck, dog Jesse, some clothes, my Bible, and my guns.
"Please God, not the guns!"

Hesitantly, I decided if God wanted my guns He could have them. I'd give them back to my Dad. But that Sunday, praise God, our pastor introduced himself to me with, "Hey, I hear you're the hunter, would you take me some time?"

Hallelujah! I kept the guns.

Sometimes God asks us to live radically. The key to being a radical for God is being willing to trust His promises. Abraham ruthlessly trusted the God who said, "Through Isaac your descendants shall be named" (Genesis 21:12).

Weigh God's powerful whisper against His perfect Word to decipher His will. Be careful about hearing God's voice in your selfishness such as, "God wants me to buy a bigger house." Don't lose sight of God in your selfishness. Be ready for the tests to come. God loves to test men.

He tested His Son (Matthew 4:1-11). He tested David (Psalm 139:23).

He will test you.

He may even ask you to raise your knife in a sacrificial offering to His will. Will you do it? Will you pass the test?

# SACRIFICE OF PRESENCE

*This is how God showed his love among us: He sent his one and only Son into the world that we might live through him.*
~ 1 John 4:9

I once spoke with a young man who showed all the signs of being fatherless. I was surprised to hear his dad was still at home. Four years later, I looked forward to finally meeting dad at his son's scholarship night. But his dad was strangely absent. He was a no-show. The young man excused away his disappointment with, "He's just shy, but I know he loves me."

Absenteeism is a strange way to show love, don't you think?

His love looked a lot like hate to me. Focus on the Family Founder, James Dobson, once said, "Love is spelled t.i.m.e. Hate then must be spelled g.o.n.e."

Love shows up. Hate is absent.

Wouldn't you love to talk to this guy? "Suck it up! Be a father! Be a man!" To make things worse, this man was a professing "Christian." He carried the title of dad, attended church regularly, but remained absent, idle, neutral. He lacked the potency and impact needed to be a Father and a man.

Sadly, churches are filled with men like this. Men who believe the lie that love is found only in the words, "I love you." But those are just words. Love is so much more.
It's sacrifice. It's presence. It's showing up.

Love serves. Love manifests. Love responds. Love acts. Love doesn't reciprocate sacrifice for sacrifice, gift for gift, but acts first. It doesn't sit on the couch, take a nap, and read a book. It acts. Translated: manhood requires the sacrifice of presence for the benefit of those you say you love.

Who are you sacrificing for? Who do you love?
Men show up.

# MARBLE BUCK

*He is the atoning sacrifice for our sins and not only for ours but also for the sins of the whole world.*
~ 1 John 2:2

Early in the morning we glassed the adjacent ridge that we called the "Hell Hole" when "Big" Darby excitedly whispered, "There's one! It's a buck!"

Most hunters have rules. Spoken, or not, these rules are designed to save friendships during tense hunting moments. One such rule is, "Whoever draws first blood gets the animal." Another is, "Whoever spots the buck has the first shot." So, when Darby spotted the buck my heart momentarily sank.

My finger wouldn't touch the trigger this morning, though I'd work just as hard and sweat just as much. But something happened. Darby looked over, smiled, and whispered, "Why don't you take this one Jimmy."

It was one of my most memorable hunting experiences. A short sneak, one shot from my Weatherby, and the Marble Buck was mine. Which brings us to today.

I'm awestruck by the differences in translation between 1 John 2:2 in the NIV and NASB. The New International Version reads, "He is the atoning sacrifice for our sins."

The New American Standard Bible is quite different; "He himself is the propitiation (or satisfaction) for our sins." The sacrifice of Jesus is literally the satisfaction for "the sins of the whole world."

For every great sacrifice there must be an equal satisfaction. Darby sacrificed his chance at the "Marble Buck" for my personal satisfaction. A man sacrifices his time and resources to satisfy the opportunity of a better life for his family. Laymen sacrifice their time and resources to satisfy God's vision for the local church.

Bring some kind of satisfaction to those you lead through personal sacrifice. Lead from the back, so others can go ahead.

# TEAM MEETING SIX: PROTECT HER

> *"Integrity is keeping my commitment even if the circumstances when I made the commitment have changed."*
> ~ David Jeremiah

**What did you take away from last week's study and daily readings? What are you still processing? What challenged your current paradigm? What inspired you to grow as a man?**

Men are like steel thermos mugs. Women are like a coffee cup made from the finest piece of china. Both serve a similar purpose. The difference is in the handling. The thermos is tough, utilitarian— built to handle the worst circumstances. The china cup is highly honored, fragile, and used on special occasions. We, as men, need to treat our wives with honor, like the china cup, not rough and tumble, like the thermos.

**Let's take a moment and share one thing you are doing to protect your (future) wife/ marriage?**

**In modern wedding ceremonies, the father of the bride "gives" his daughter to her soon-to-be-husband in a symbolic passing of the mantle of leadership. The new husband becomes the provider, spiritual leader, and nurturer of his bride. What do the following verses teach us about protecting our (future) wife?**
Genesis 2:23-25, Matthew 19:4-6, and Ephesians 5:25-32

# TEAM MEETING AT A GLANCE
- Opening Prayer, Weekly Announcements
- Personal and Victory Stories
- Each man will share his story — one man per week until all men have shared.
- After all men have shared their personal story, allow time each week for them to share victory stories.
- Weekly Study Closing Prayer
- Closing Prayer

> *"The key to powerful manhood is that a man fully owns—takes responsibility for, tends, stands guard over, assures the healthy condition of—the field assigned to him."*
> ~ Steven Mansfield

*The man said, "This is now bone of my bones and flesh of my flesh; she shall be called 'woman,' for she was taken out of man." That is why a man leaves his father and mother and is united to his wife, and they become one flesh. Adam and his wife were both naked, and they felt no shame.*
~ Genesis 2:23-25

**Last week we discussed guardrails. What guardrails have you implemented to prevent you from veering off course into sin? What guardrails challenge you?**

The wise build guardrails around themselves and those they love. The art of prevention, of navigating away from the edge, is more important than vision. It is vision! Relationships, marriages, and careers crash when men fail to steer away from the edge. Develop the art of staying as far away from the edge as possible.

**We live in a day where lust is celebrated. How does lust manifest itself in your life? How can lust affect the marriage covenant? What do you do to protect yourself from it?**
Psalm 119:9-11, Matthew 5:27-30, Hebrews 13:4, and 1 Peter 2:11

> *"Manhood at its most basic level can be validated and expressed only in action."*
> ~ George Gilder

Lock arms with men you trust. Protecting your wife and those you love from the collateral damage of your secret sins takes a team of trusted men-a band of brothers.

**What covenant have you made with your eyes about looking at women lustfully? What roles do you live by that protect your marriage from lust? Who else are you locking arms within this battle?**
Exodus 20:17, Job 31:1-4, and Psalm 101:2-3

A smartphone that is not protected against pornography belongs to a dumb man.

**What advice can we gather from 2 Timothy 2:22?**

*Flee the evil desires of youth and pursue righteousness, faith, love and peace, along with those who call on the Lord out of a pure heart.*
*~ 2 Timothy 2:22*

**How does the single man (unmarried, divorced, or widower) protect his future wife?**

**What is the Bible's stance for a man—single, married, widowed, and divorced—when it comes to protecting his (future) wife?**
1 Corinthians 6:9-20 and 1 Thessalonians 4:3-8

Venus was the Roman goddess of love and beauty. She was the principal deity of the city of Corinth when Paul wrote both letters to the Corinthian Church. Her temple was one of the most magnificent in the city and hosted 1000 priestesses to Venus.

These "priestesses" were publicly supported prostitutes that offered their services at any time to the worship of the god Venus.

**What do the following verses teach about sex, love, and marriage?**
Proverbs 5:18-20 and Song of Songs 7:7-9

> *Show me a man you honor, and I will know what kind of man you are, for it shows me what your ideal of manhood is and what kind of man you long to be."*
> ~ Thomas Carlyle

Extreme foreplay involves oral sex, toys, or any forms of sex without actual penetration.

**Here's a loaded question that may take some time to discuss. You may want to hold off until another meeting, but it needs to be discussed eventually. What can you find from today's study or elsewhere in Scripture about masturbation, co-habitation (outside of marriage), and extreme foreplay (outside of marriage)?**
Matthew 5:27-32

> *"It is amazing that a single 'Christian' man, called to protect his woman, will choose to live with her, have regular sex, and generally test drive the relationship while the Christian community looks on. This same man will call himself a committed follower of Jesus and protector of his woman's reputation. Huh?"*
> ~ Jim Ramos

*If your right eye causes you to stumble, gouge it out and throw it away. It is better for you to lose one part of your body than for your whole body to be thrown into hell. And if your right hand causes you to stumble, cut it off and throw it away. It is better for you to lose one part of your body than for your whole body to go into hell.*
~ Matthew 5:29-31

Break into groups of three or four.

**Where are you struggling with sexual purity?**

Take a moment today and pray for each other.

# STUDY NOTES

_____
_____
_____
_____
_____
_____
_____
_____
_____
_____
_____
_____
_____
_____
_____
_____

For the next five days, read the following entries from our **The Field Guide: A Bathroom Book for Men.**

We hope they challenge and encourage you to get in the great Arena for God. See you on the Arena Floor!

# EMASCULATED MAN

*Even though I walk through the valley of the shadow of death, I will fear no evil, for you are with me; your rod and your staff, they comfort me. You prepare a table before me in the presence of my enemies.*
~ Psalm 23:4-5

A good friend told me, "Everyone I talk to knows you." He smirked then continued, "Some people really like you. Others, not so much."

He was referring to a mutual acquaintance that pulled her son from my team because I was too hard on the boys. Our conversation ended with her sarcastic exclamation, "Well, I guess I don't understand because I'm a woman!"

She was exactly right. She didn't.

Our culture has emasculated men into believing the lie that they should settle quietly into a life of passivity and let others lead them. As a generation, we've become soft. Impotent. Is passivity the cross Jesus calls men to carry?

No.

Impotence is the result of a man who's surrendered his jewels to a society holding the rusted blade. Unfortunately, the passive man is in the majority, and the assertive man is becoming a dying breed. Passivity has television networks, but assertiveness stands alone.

It's easier to watch Eve eat the forbidden fruit than to rip it out of her hand, push her aside, and crush the serpent's head.

Too many men fear their enemies to the point of having none. Aren't enemies the only ones who have the guts to tell us the truth? Aren't they the ones who publicly stand against us? If you stand for something, those opposing his God will stand in defiance.

Should he cower before them, unwilling to "piss anyone off"? Or should he stand and engage a culture that has turned on men?

# STUMBLING BLOCKS

*Do not curse the deaf or put a stumbling block in front of the blind, but fear your God. I am the Lord.*
~ Leviticus 19:14

I vividly remember the few times Dad hunted me down with a BB gun. It wouldn't have been so bad, but he was a pretty good shot. On several occasions, Dad's friends came over, grabbed the BB guns, and gave us kids the evil smirk, "Run!"

It was The Hunger Games in real-time.

Today's passage addresses a major issue in contemporary Christianity. It's the issue of how we, as men, handle our freedom in Christ. Abraham Lincoln once said, "If you want to test a man's character, give him power." If you want to really test a man, give him freedom."

How does the lender handle the one who owes him money? How does the boss handle his employee? How does the shepherd handle the sheep? How do the rich handle the poor? How do the strong handle the weak? How does a man handle his children?

It would be easy to "put a stumbling block in front of " those we have power or authority over without regard for their dignity in each situation. This is wrong. Immaturity is often masked as arrogance that disregards another's temptations for personal freedom.

How we handle our freedom in Christ says a lot about integrity. It says a lot about how much a man fears God and loves his neighbor.

The mature follower of Jesus is acutely aware of the issues and bondages of those around him. He doesn't use his freedom as an excuse to sin but a reason to love.

He recognizes the stumbling blocks all around and vows never to be one of them. He's mature. He fears God.

# WINNING

*So I continued, "What you are doing is not right. Shouldn't you walk in the fear of our God to avoid the reproach of our Gentile enemies?"*
~ Nehemiah 5:9

I grew up in a highly competitive world. Sports and the outdoors were part of my childhood. I realized God had given me some athletic abilities early on, but my competitive spirit was over the top. I despised losing and would go to extremes for a win. Defeating the opponent consumed me, which was humiliating since we lost more than we won—way more.

One Friday night under the lights, an opposing team had a great player who punished me. I couldn't stop him. I didn't know what to do but saw my opportunity when he lined up on my inside gap for a field goal. Shamefully, I chop blocked him and took him out of the game.

We still lost.

After finding Christ, however, my dysfunctional paradigm of winning was slowly replaced with a Biblical model. The focus shifted from battling against an opponent to fighting to please an audience of One.

The opponent ceased to be an enemy and was replaced by a desire to please God. Honoring God became the goal, and with it, a Biblical understanding of winning.

Nehemiah lived according to this paradigm of winning. He admonished men to "walk in the fear of God." Walking in fear of God's opponents is a non-issue when our greatest desire is to please God. The true enemy of a man is the guy he shaves with. If he can defeat the man in the mirror, he'll please his King.

# CLEAN YOUR GUN

*The fear of the Lord is clean, enduring forever; the judgments of the Lord are true; they are righteous altogether.*
~ Psalm 19:9 (NASB)

Ruger 10/22 rifles are famous for their innumerable aftermarket accessories. I was handed down two and gave one to my son, Darby. We decided to accessorize them, creating a cool new look with each gun.

But these rifles have a problem. Extreme carbon builds up from shooting hundreds of rounds can gum them up, creating a jam. It's a challenge to keep the inside mechanisms clean, so the outside performs well.

Darby's gun was so gummed up from years of neglect we were surprised it could even fire until he finally cleaned it. The inside affects the outside.

The New American Standard translation of Psalm 19:9 is interesting, "The fear of the Lord is clean, enduring forever." A man who fears God desires to live a clean and pure life. This deep conviction compels him to maintain his heart, so the inside matches the outside. He keeps his gun clean.

Remember when Jesus rebuked some religious men, "Woe to you, teachers of the law and Pharisees, you hypocrites! You are like whitewashed tombs, which look beautiful on the outside but on the inside are full of dead men's bones and everything unclean" (Matthew 23:27).

There's no need to pretend to play church or put on a superficial Sunday smile with the man who fears God. He keeps his gun clean. The inside matches the outside. The public self reflects the private self. He keeps his gun clean.

"Blessed are the pure in heart, for they will see God" (Matthew 5:8).

# HEATSTROKE BUCK

*But may all who seek you rejoice and be glad in you; may those who love your salvation always say,*
*"Let God be exalted!"*
~ Psalm 70:4

When my college football career was over, I was excited to finally enjoy a full deer season. Playing football cut deer hunting season in half.

You can imagine my enthusiasm the first morning of my first full deer season since childhood. After a steep one-mile hike, I spotted a nice buck, killing him on the third shot. He expired in the bottom of a west-facing canyon.

I was keenly aware of the eastern sun rising over the ridge, preparing to uncover its mid-morning wrath. Racing against it, I pulled the dead weight over, under, through the brush, and out of the canyon.

The closer I got to the top, the more the sun beat down until I was spent. My legs swelled beyond the capacity of my Wranglers, causing cramping. The temperature neared one hundred degrees, and it was barely ten o'clock.

I ran out of water.

I was in trouble.

I wished I were in the heat of double-day football practices. I knew the deer would soon spoil, but I was in serious trouble of soiling if I didn't cool down and drink something soon.

Fortunately, Dad and Grandpa spotted me and came to my rescue. With their help, I survived, and the buck didn't spoil. It was a good day—barely!

Have you ever been in a situation that could've gone either way? Did you know your soul could be divided? Do you know Who came to rescue your soul?

"Enter through the narrow gate. For wide is the gate and broad is the road that leads to destruction, and many enter through it. But small is the gate and narrow the road that leads to life, and only a few find it"(Matthew 7:13-14).

Live for Jesus today and every day. Start now.

# TEAM MEETING SEVEN: WHO OWNS YOU?

> *"To forgive is to set a prisoner free, only to realize that prisoner is you."*
> ~ Corrie ten Boom

**What did you take away from last week's study and daily readings? What are you still processing? What challenged your current paradigm? What inspired you to grow as a man?**

**How much do your words reflect the true you? How do your words express your heart to those around you? What do your words tell others about your relationship with God?**

Our words express one of three things: our freedom, lack of self-control, or inability to forgive.

**Verse 2 of James chapter 3 makes a bold statement about the ability to control our words. If a man can control his words, what else can he control? Explain.**

We all stumble in many ways. Anyone who is never at fault in what they say is perfect, able to keep their whole body in check.

**James 3:1-12 is titled "Taming the Tongue." What do "bits into horses' mouths" (verse 3), ships "steered by a very small rudder" (verse 4), and "a great forest is set on fire by a small spark" (verse 5) teach us about the power of words?**

# TEAM MEETING AT A GLANCE

- Opening Prayer, Weekly Announcements
- Personal and Victory Stories
- Each man will share his story — one man per week until all men have shared.
- After all men have shared their personal story, allow time each week for them to share victory stories.
- Weekly Study Closing Prayer
- Closing Prayer

*"To be a Christian means to forgive the inexcusable because God has forgiven the inexcusable in you."*
~ C.S. Lewis

**Last week we discussed guardrails. What guardrails have you implemented to prevent you from veering off course into sin? What guardrails challenge you?**

**How do our words about another person reflect our heart, relationship, or bitterness to them?**

Words are powerful. They are either a powerful building tool or a deadly weapon of destruction. As the spiritual leader, your words teach those you love how to live a life set apart for God with words, attitudes, and actions.

**Do the things we say originate in the darkness of our hearts or from a lack of mental discipline? Are our words a head or heart issue? Can you explain the discrepancy between the following verses?**
Matthew 12:34-37, Romans 12:1-2, 2 Corinthians 10:3-6, and James 1:26

**We tend to be ledger people. We tend to keep score. But Jesus doesn't keep score. He forgives. How do your words reflect unforgiveness, bitterness, or resentment towards someone else?**

Anger, bitterness, resentment, and maliciousness are signs of an unforgiving heart. Our unwillingness to find freedom through forgiveness enables the offender in question to own us due to a lack of forgiveness. Sadly, the offender often doesn't even know there's a problem. Ironically the offender is the last person on the planet we want to lay claim to our heart, but they own us nonetheless. But now you're sharing a piece of your heart with them and Jesus. Essentially, your resentment towards an offender puts them on the throne right next to God.

**Based on your words, who owns you? Who are you in bondage to? Who do your words most often condemn? Who do you find yourself thinking hateful thoughts towards? Who do you gossip the most about?**

**A good test to see if someone owns you is to ask yourself what comes to mind when you see or hear his or her name?**

*If you love those who love you, what credit is that to you? Even sinners love those who love them. And, if you do good to those who are good to you, what credit is that to you? Even sinners do that. And if you lend to those from whom you expect repayment, what credit is that to you? Even sinners lend to sinners, expecting to be repaid in full. But love your enemies, do good to them, and lend to them without expecting to get anything back. Then your reward will be great..."*
*~ Luke 6:32-35*

**How does God handle our offenses, our sins, against Him?**
Isaiah 1:18, Matthew 26:27-28, Ephesians 1:6-8, Colossians 1:13-14, 2 Corinthians 5:21, Hebrews 8:12, James 5:15 and 1 Peter 3:18

**God forgives us of the worst of sins. You can imagine the paradox when God's people refuse to forgive. What did Jesus mean with such a radical claim about forgiveness in Matthew 6:14-15? Was he serious? Was he using hyperbole?**

*For if you forgive other people when they sin against you, your heavenly Father will also forgive you. But if you do not forgive others their sins, your Father will not forgive your sins.*
*~ Matthew 6:14-15*

**Matthew 18:21-35 is The Parable of the Unmerciful Servant. What do we learn about the power of forgiveness? How do you relate to this? Can you put verses 21-22 into your own words?**

The problem with unforgiveness is that we surrender our freedom in Christ to it. We exchange the ability to love God with all our heart, mind, soul, and strength for anger, resentment, bitterness, and rage. The person (or people) who wounded you lay claim to a piece of your heart until you release them through forgiveness.

They become idols that you worship through hate. God is jealous for all your heart, and He deserves to have it all.

**Forgiveness is a process. We're the ones who lose when we reject the process of forgiveness on our way back to freedom. What is the biggest obstacle we face when working our way back to freedom?**

*For I, The Lord your God, am a jealous God...."*
~ Exodus 20:5

We've built a pretty strong case for freedom through forgiveness. But how do we work through the process of forgiveness? How should we handle those who have hurt us? Are there steps we can take to find forgiveness for our offenders? As a group, use the passage below and those on to craft some steps in the forgiveness process.

*If you love those who love you, what credit is that to you? Even sinners love those who love them. And if you do good to those who are good to you, what credit is that to you? Even sinners do that. And if you lend to those from whom you expect repayment, what credit is that to you? Even sinners lend to sinners, expecting to be repaid in full. But love your enemies, do good to them, and lend to them without expecting to get anything back. Then your reward will be great...*
~ Luke 6:32-35

*Bless those who persecute you; bless and do not curse.... If it is possible, as far as it depends on you, live at peace with everyone. Do not take revenge, my dear friends, but leave room for God's wrath, for it is written: "It is mine to avenge; I will repay," says the Lord. On the contrary: "If your enemy is hungry, feed him; if he is thirsty, give him something to drink. In doing this, you will heap burning coals on his head." Do not be overcome by evil, but overcome evil with good.*
~ Romans 12:14 and 18-21

*Finally, all of you, be like-minded, be sympathetic, love one another, be compassionate and humble. Do not repay evil with evil or insult with insult. On the contrary, repay evil with blessing, because to this you were called so that you may inherit a blessing. For, "Whoever would love life and see good days must keep their tongue from evil and their lips from deceitful speech*
~ 1 Peter 3:8-10

**What is a godly solution for your words when someone hurts you?**

**Break into groups of three or four. Is there a person that needs your forgiveness today?**

**How can we pray for your offender today?**

Take a moment today and pray for each other.

# STUDY NOTES

_____
_____
_____
_____
_____
_____
_____
_____
_____
_____
_____
_____
_____
_____

For the next five days, read the following entries from our **The Field Guide: A Bathroom Book for Men.**

We hope they challenge and encourage you to get in the great Arena for God. See you on the Arena Floor!

# LAUGH AT FEAR

*He laughs at fear, afraid of nothing; he does not shy away from the sword.*
~ Job 39:22

Have you ever heard a man say, "I laugh at fear."? I've never heard a woman say it, but I've heard men on numerous occasions. Why is it that when men are faced with great danger, they casually shrug it off?

Fear is nothing to be laughed at. Fear is a wet-your-pants moment. Fear is what I call a "pucker" moment. Fear is never something to mock or tease, and especially laugh at.

Then, who is this mighty warrior in Job 39:22 who "laughs at fear, afraid of nothing."? This is someone you definitely want on your side when walking down a dark alley.

This is someone to be reckoned with, wouldn't you agree? Verse 20 gives the answer: "Do you give the horse his might? Do you clothe his neck with a mane? Do you make him leap like the locust?" (NASB)

That's right; God is talking about a horse. In other words, no man laughs at fear.

Three times in verse 20, God asks, "Do you give, clothe, or make?" Only he can create certain things, and one of those things is fearlessness. No matter how strong or courageous, all men fear at some point. But God can help in gaining victory over our fears.

The same God who made the horse laugh at fear is the same God who gives men victory over it. Stop lying about laughing at fear. Instead, embrace it; admit it to others while moving forward.

Be like young David against Goliath.

Pick up some polished stones, place one in the sling and start throwing!

# WHAT YOU PAY FOR

*The Lord also will be a stronghold for the oppressed, a stronghold in times of trouble; and those who know Your name will put their trust in you, for you, O Lord, have not forsaken those who seek you.*
~ Psalms 9:9-10 (NASB)

I camped with a one-man bivouac tent that weighed less than four pounds and cost less than fifty bucks for years. It sounds like a great deal until I learned the hard way you get what you pay for.

I ended up caught in a snowstorm at 8,000 feet elevation. The tent began to drift up with snow. Though concealed under a small conifer grove, I was forced to use an emergency space blanket to make a lean-to in order to prevent its total collapse, which turned out to be a lifesaver.

Today's passage speaks about God's covering during times of trouble. Bad things happen. But when our shelter is compromised, bad things get worse. A stronghold is a guard from the forces that beat us down. It covers us when we're not strong enough to weather the storms ourselves. God protects those who trust His covering.

A lean-to protects an object by leaning away from the storm. God covers those who lean away from the storms of life and into Him. To seek God is to move in God's direction and under His cover. To trust Him is to allow Him to shelter every aspect of your life.

"Trust in the Lord with all your heart and lean not on your own understanding; in all your ways acknowledge him, and he will make your paths straight" (Proverbs 3:5-6).
Did you see that? Where have you leaned into fair-weather shelters? Where have you leaned the wrong way?

Lean into the God who covers, especially during life's many storms.

# WINNING BIG

*Though I am free and belong to no man, I make myself a slave to everyone, to win as many as possible.*
~ 1 Corinthians 9:19

A parent once called to inform me that his son quit the team because of my unrealistic expectations for the players. Though he didn't use the word, my interpretation was that we demanded too much. His son was a good player, and I lost him.

As a follower of Jesus, I grieved that loss as a personal failure. I later apologized to the young man for failing him as his coach. It served as another defining moment.

Failure can be that moment of truth when we learn winning isn't the end in itself. It's only a tool. Any talent or passion that God gives should draw others to Him and not repulse them. This was why I apologized. I failed Christ more than the young man.

There are no higher stakes on earth than forever. We can't reclaim it. We only have one shot. We must be careful to influence people towards that end and not repulse them.

Too often, I hear of Christians who are hated by their associates, and I wonder how they got to that point? Did they forget that life is only a tool?

"You're telling me he's a %^&*(#@ Christian!?"

When I forget who I'm representing, I become harsh and critical. I become everything I don't want to be, unlike Paul, who said, "I have become all things to all men so that by all possible means I might save some. I do all this for the sake of the gospel, that I may share in its blessings" (1 Corinthians 9:22).

I am tempted to become "all things" for the sake of personal gain and not the glory of God.

It's in those moments I remember who I work for and act accordingly.

# CHIP OFF THE BLOCK

*Listen to me, you who pursue righteousness and who seek the Lord: Look to the rock from which you were cut and to the quarry from which you were hewn.*
~ Isaiah 51:1

Years ago, I met with a young man who was leaving town hoping to join an elite military unit. In his sophomore year, we were close, but I saw him less and less the closer he got to graduation. By the time he graduated, I rarely saw him. After working with students most of my adult life,

I've learned that youth ministry is about delayed gratification. As teens mature into adulthood, they begin to appreciate those who locked arms with them during their formative years.

All of us are the product of the investment of others. Sadly, some are the product of key men who failed them during the formative years of life. What should be the fruit of one's labor becomes collateral damage when a man fails.

Think about the coaches, teachers, family members, mentors, or ministers whose example (good, bad, or ugly) influenced the man you are today. You are a chip off the old block of the men who were in, or absent from, your life. You may have a chip on your shoulder or be a chip off the old block: either way, there's a chip.

In Isaiah 51:1, God is described as our rock and our foundation. He's our creator and designer. He desires His men to be a chip off the Rock. This reminds me of a poster I had in my college dorm. It was a picture of men, nearly hidden within the immensity of a huge rock formation. The poster's caption was Psalm 61:2, "Lead me to the rock that is higher than I."

You are created for a high calling. You are made in the image of your Creator (Genesis 1:26). Is there a chip on your shoulder from a man who let you down?

If so, knock it off. You're a chip off the Rock

# REDNECK CIRCLE

*Seek the Lord, all you humble of the land, you who do what he commands. Seek righteousness, seek humility; perhaps you will be sheltered on the day of the Lord's anger.*
~ Zephaniah 2:3

I grew up in redneck circles. I was raised around men who loved to hunt, fish, and spend time outdoors. This book is the way it is because it's who I am. Like it or not, I really don't care.

I'm a Redneck.

An unwritten code in Redneck circles is you must be found worthy of being called a Redneck. Bragging is one way of earning your place in the circle. But there's an even better, sneakier way to enter the circle. It is to simply ask another Redneck to teach you something. Seek his advice and enter the Redneck realm by default.

Wait, maybe that's true for all of us. We love to be respected as experts.

Respect is the greatest gift one man can give another.

Humility is an endangered species in the circle of men these days.

Humility stands out like a suit and tie in the midst of Wranglers and Carharts. Those who don't ask questions don't get answers. Those who don't get answers don't grow. Those who don't grow don't experience the joy of success that humility brings.

As Zephaniah states, a person can't be "humble" if that person won't

"seek the Lord." To seek the Lord is to admit we are lesser, and He is greater. John the Baptist nailed it: "He must become greater; I must become less" (John 3:30). When a man seeks the Lord, he's acknowledging that God is greater. He is lesser.

When a man doesn't seek the Lord during those seasons, he'll seek other sources for guidance. But God's commands are better than any of man's solutions. Get off your high horse of pride and step away from the Redneck circle long enough to realize this—you're not God.

# TEAM MEETING EIGHT: THE EXAMPLE

> *"It is impossible to ask your son to do something you cannot model for him. He has a large radar dish on his head that hears hypocrisy."*
> ~ William Beausay,
> Boys: Shaping Ordinary Boys into Extraordinary Men

**What did you take away from last week's study and daily readings? What are you still processing? What challenged your current paradigm? What inspired you to grow as a man?**

**Let's all answer this question: What would your co-workers tell us about your Christian example in the workplace?**

God is not one of the compartments in our hectic lives that we dedicate an hour or so of our time to and forget about. He must permeate into all aspects of life until we are the same man in every situation. God doesn't want any part of you. He wants every part of you.

**How do you model your faith to your family? How is Jesus our role model? What is Jesus saying in the passage below? What are some other examples that Jesus left behind?**

# TEAM MEETING AT A GLANCE

- Opening Prayer, Weekly Announcements
- Personal and Victory Stories
- Each man will share his story — one man per week until all men have shared.
- After all men have shared their personal story, allow time each week for them to share victory stories.
- Weekly Study Closing Prayer
- Closing Prayer

> *"Few things are harder to put up with than the annoyance of a good example."*
> ~ Mark Twain

*12 When he had finished washing their feet, he put on his clothes and returned to his place. "Do you understand what I have done for you?" he asked them.*
*13 "You call me 'Teacher' and 'Lord,' and rightly so, for that is what I am. 14 Now that I, your Lord and Teacher, have washed your feet, you also should wash one another's feet. 15 I have set you an example that you should do as I have done for you.16 Very truly I tell you, no servant is greater than his master, nor is a messenger greater than the one who sent him.17 Now that you know these things, you will be blessed if you do them.*
John 13:12-17

What positive example have you set for those closest to you? At the end of the day, don't be as interested in being an example of a good man as you are about being a Godhunter—a man chasing after God.

**What negative example have you set that needs to be addressed? Check out the lyrics from Rodney Atkins' country song, Watching You. Based on those, what are the take-away for us as spiritual leaders?**

> *Let not him who is houseless pull down the house of another, but let him work diligently and build one for himself, thus by example assuring that his own shall be safe from violence when built.*
> ~ Abraham Lincoln

*How are you modeling Christ to others? How are you pointing others to Him with your actions? What comparison is the Apostle Paul making to others? What can we learn about our battle to be examples of biblical manhood in a world with a contrary view?*
~ Philippians 3:15-21

**What are some other ways you can be an example of biblical manhood? Why is it so important to have an intergenerational focus with modeling our faith?**
Thessalonians 1:6-8, 2 Thessalonians 3:6-12, 1 Timothy 4:11-16, and Titus 2:6-8

> *"There are old heads in the world who cannot help me by their example or advice to live worthily and satisfactorily to myself, but I believe that it is in my power to elevate myself this very hour above the common level of my life."*
> ~ Henry David Thoreau

**What does the Bible teach us about secret sin? What happens when our public persona and private life are not in alignment?**
Psalm 90:8, 94:8-11, 139:1-6, Ephesians 5:12, Luke 12:2-3 and James 5:16

A true role model is the same man in public as he is in private.

**How does hypocrisy hinder your Christian example?**
Timothy 4:1-4 and Revelation 3:14-21

There is no such thing as a lukewarm follower of Jesus. There are only lukewarm "Christians." The word "Christian" has been abused for so long that it's become synonymous with American, Conservative, and good person. But are you a follower of Jesus? No one is perfect, but the lukewarm are most often credited with hypocrisy.

**Break into groups of three or four. Rethink the example you're setting at work, home, and in social settings. What needs to change? Take a moment today and pray for each other.**

# STUDY NOTES

_____
_____
_____
_____
_____
_____
_____
_____
_____
_____
_____
_____
_____
_____
_____

For the next five days, read the following entries from our **The Field Guide: A Bathroom Book for Men.**

We hope they challenge and encourage you to get in the great Arena for God. See you on the Arena Floor!

# ANXIETY AND JOY

*Do not grieve, for the joy of the LORD is your strength.*
Nehemiah 8:10

*I have learned the secret of being content in any and every situation, whether well fed or hungry, whether living in plenty or in want.*
~ Philippians 4:12

To compensate for my lack of problem-solving skills during a crisis, I prepare for every possible contingency. For example, when exploring the backcountry, I take great pains to assemble all the food, water, heat, and shelter I may need.

Oh, did I forget to mention coffee?

The mystery of the wilderness can be either a source of great anxiety or overwhelming joy. Knowing this, I prepare against anxiety to experience maximum joy.

Paul's adult life was spent traveling in wilderness areas of the northern Mediterranean Sea and southern Asia. He couldn't stop at a hotel and rent a luxury suite. He couldn't take a heated car or train. He couldn't book a flight.

He walked.

The road was often treacherous. Can you imagine?

But his strength came from knowing God would protect him regardless of the many dangers along the way. Paul ruthlessly trusted God.

Trusting God daily is a great struggle for contemporary men living in our consumeristic world. Preparing for the day is more than grabbing your cell phone, credit card, and car keys on the way out the door. It's about the contentment that comes from taking the time to be with God in Word and prayer.

Joy doesn't just happen. It's the fruit of the man who places his trust in Jesus through all that life throws his way (Galatians 5:22).

# WEAKNESS THROUGH NEGLECT

*For my life is spent with sorrow, and my years with sighing; my strength has failed because of my iniquity, and my body has wasted away.*
~ Psalm 31:10 (NASB)

When the Santa Clara Broncos football players rolled in for fall camp, there was always a buzz about who showed up looking good and who had been obviously slacking. Those who neglected summer workouts were usually softer, slower, and weaker. Their lack of fitness not only hurt themselves but the team.

The psalmist was right about sin when he wrote, "My strength has failed because of my iniquity."

Sin weakens a man.

It robs his youthfulness, strength, and energy. When he's up late watching ESPN, browsing the Internet, or gaming instead of getting that extra hour of sleep, he wakes up tired, weak, and soft.

Take my Achilles Heel, for example—food.

Gluttons are more prone to gout, asthma, indigestion, heart disease, Type II diabetes, and many other diet-related infirmities. Those who misuse tobacco are at risk for cancer, not to mention early aging and the infamous "smoker's voice." Drinking too much alcohol can lead to liver damage, life damage, and a poor Christian witness. We could go on and on about vices such as drugs, pride, pornography, and greed.

A good measuring rod of sin's negative affect is to monitor your strength throughout the day. Strength is a great measuring rod against sin because sin weakens a man. Sin is greedy. It wants more. Sin kills (Romans 6:23). Sin is the crease in our armor. Sin is the weakest link. Sin not only has spiritual ramifications but obvious physical ones.

Where has sin weakened you?

# GRAY HAIR OF GLORY

*The glory of young men is their strength, gray hair the splendor of the old.*
~ Proverbs 20:29

I recently added Bob Seger's classic hit song Like a Rock to my song list. There's something about that song that brings tears to my middle-aged eyes. Entering the second half of life, I wish I could tell our younger men to live their dreams and honor those who've dreamt before them. I'd tell them to find wiser, older men to be their compass.

A young man boasts in the strength of his youth. At the same time, older men are bidding strength farewell. But don't discount the older men just yet. They've more to offer than you could ever imagine. They have something neither strength nor money can buy—wisdom.

Have you noticed who young men work for? That's right, the older men.

I can't tell you how many times Dad strolled through the woods watching me drag or carry his buck to the truck. Younger men can learn a lot from their older mentors.

Wisdom works smarter, not harder. Find an older man to honor as your mentor. Who are the gray (or baldheads) in your life that you can lean into for wisdom and strength?

# PULL-UPS

*This is what the Lord says: "Let not the wise man boast of his wisdom or the strong man boast of his strength or the rich man boast of his riches, but let him who boasts boast about this: that he understands and knows me, that I am the Lord, who exercises kindness, justice, and righteousness on earth, for in these I delight," declares the Lord.*
~ Jeremiah 9:23-24

A pull-up competition broke out at summer camp one year, and each of the high school students stepped up to the cabin's beam to make their best attempt. After watching several and knowing it was now or never, I jumped to the beam with adrenaline pumping and completed the ugliest twenty pull-ups ever recorded.

I stuck out my chest and began to talk a little smack to my wide-eyed students. Just then, a lead counselor, half my weight, completed twenty-two perfect pull-ups, much easier than my ugly twenty.

Besides humility, I learned a lesson that night. I'm incredibly blessed. God has taken care of me and given me good things. One of these things is a strong body. My response to this is to acknowledge the blessing and deflect the boasting.

Listen to the wisdom of Paul's words in 1 Corinthians 4:7-8: "For who makes you different from anyone else? What do you have that you did not receive? And if you did receive it, why do you boast as though you did not? Already you have all you want! Already you have become rich!"

The proper response to God's blessings is to brag about the Blesser more than the blessing. As men, our tendency is to talk smack, pump up our chest, and brag. This is the wrong response to God's blessings.

When others want to put our accomplishments on display, the proper response is to put Jesus on display instead.

# HOLD IT

*But Christ is faithful as a son over God's house. And we are his house, if we hold on to our courage and the hope of which we boast.*
~ Hebrews 3:6

One of the most influential studies in my life was the exhaustive study of the word courage in the Bible. This is one of them. At the time, I sensed God leading to a place that would take great courage. I didn't know that courage would be needed to move my young family from California to Oregon in a few months.

A decade later, we needed more courage to step out in faith to pioneer a new ministry during a bad economy, with no support and little hope of success—Men in the Arena.

From this study, I had one major takeaway. Here it is. Courage must be taken. It isn't something you receive. It's not a fruit of the Spirit. It's not a spiritual gift. It's not a talent. It's not one of the Ten Commandments, nor any of the 613 rules of Mosaic Law. Courage must be taken (1 Samuel 4:9).

Courage challenges the status quo.

Courage isn't a feeling either. It's often a response contrary to our feelings. Actually, courage is often birthed out of fear. Men either rise to meet the challenge of their fears or fall into cowardice.

Courage acts. Cowardice surrenders.

Courage is the response to our faith. When fear manifests itself, courage moves forward in a ruthless act of trust. Unlike a spiritual gift, talent, or fruit of the Spirit, courage is one thing God asks men to choose—to take (Psalm 31:24).

Taking courage isn't enough. It must be held onto once it's been taken. Today's courageous men can be tomorrow's cowards if they don't ferociously grip courage.

The more of the world we hold, the more difficult it is to keep our grip on courage, which often slips through our fingers. Hold onto it every day, all the time.

Hold courage. Never let it go (Acts 23:11).

# TEAM MEETING NINE: GET TO WORK

> *"Get going. Move forward. Aim High. Plan a takeoff. Don't just sit on the runway and hope someone will come along and push the airplane."*
> ~ Donald J. Trump

**What did you take away from last week's study and daily readings? What are you still processing? What challenged your current paradigm? What inspired you to grow as a man? Discuss the statement, "What you do (for work) does not define who you are."**

**The two most important questions in life are: Who am I? Why am I here? How do you see these questions creating confusion for men? Who are you? Have you ever stopped to think about your identity? Where does it come from? What drives your life? If all hell broke loose in your life, what would anchor you? Again, who are you?**
Romans 8:14-17, Galatians 3:26-29,, Ephesians 2:1-10, and Colossians 3:1-4.

There are 272 Bible results for the words "in Christ" when searched in the New International Version of the Bible through the Bible Gateway application.

**You are not what you do. But what you do matters as a witness to those around you. How should you model your work ethic as a follower of Jesus?**
Colossians 3:16-17, 22-23, and Ephesians 6:5-8

# TEAM MEETING AT A GLANCE

- Opening Prayer, Weekly Announcements
- Personal and Victory Stories
- Each man will share his story — one man per week until all men have shared.
- After all men have shared their personal story, allow time each week for them to share victory stories.
- Weekly Study Closing Prayer
- Closing Prayer

> *"When he worked, he really worked. But when he played, he really played."*
> ~ Dr. Seuss

We have one boss, and that One is not our employer. The ethical code for a follower of Jesus is to work with all your heart, all the time, even when the supervisor isn't watching.

*What's the tension between balancing a strong work ethic with modeling a dynamic faith in Jesus?*

As men, we struggle with placing our identity in Jesus ahead of our work. Isn't it interesting that the first thing we talk about when with a group of men isn't Jesus? It's our career. The problem with identifying with what we do is that careers change. This is tough when, many times, men will have spent more time at a specific job than following Christ.

**What other work principles can you gather from the following verses?**
2 Thessalonians 3:7-13, and Ephesians 4:25-32

> *"I wish to preach, not on the doctrine of ignoble ease, but the doctrine of the strenuous life, the life of toil and effort, of labor and strife; to preach that higher form of success which comes, not to a man who desires mere easy peace, but to the man who does not shrink from danger, from hardship or from bitter toil, and who out of these wins the splendid ultimate triumph."*
> ~ Theodore Roosevelt, 1899

> *"Without ambition, one starts nothing.*
> *Without work, one finishes nothing."*
> ~ Ralph Waldo Emerson

Did you notice that to this point of today's meeting that the Apostle Paul wrote all of our Bible references? When he wasn't planting churches, traveling the Mediterranean regions, and writing thirteen of the twenty-seven books of the New Testament, he was a tentmaker by trade (Acts 18:2-4).

He made tents to support his ministry. Making tents meant handling urine to soften the leather. When his hands were not praying for others, they may have been softening leather with animal urine. Paul gave us a great example of balancing work ethic and ministering to others.

How should a man balance work and family? Below are two attitudes not to have!

*"I always arrive late at the office, but I make up for it by leaving early."*
~ Charles Lamb

*"I like work: it fascinates me. I can sit and look at it for hours."*
~ Jerome K. Jerome, English writer, and humanist

**What do these other proverbs teach about work ethic?**
Proverbs 12:11, 12:14, 14:23, 16:26, 21:25, 24:27, and 28:19

> *Lazy hands make for poverty, but diligent hands bring wealth.*
> ~ Proverbs 10:4

Break into groups of two or three.

**How is your work ethic a good witness to your faith?**

**Where does your work ethic need a little work?**

Take a moment today and pray for each other.

> *"Don't mistake activity with achievement."*
> ~ John Wooden

# STUDY NOTES

For the next five days, read the following entries from our **The Field Guide: A Bathroom Book for Men.**

We hope they challenge and encourage you to get in the great Arena for God. See you on the Arena Floor!

# PULL IT OUT

*Have I not commanded you? Be strong and courageous. Do not be terrified; do not be discouraged, for the Lord your God will be with you wherever you go.*
~ Joshua 1:9

I hated onions growing up. Except for onion rings, you couldn't pay me to eat one of those things. My stepmother, Gail, had a game she'd play with the onions. She cut them so small that I could taste them but couldn't see them. Whenever I noticed, she'd say and say, "Jimmy, I put a few in but cut them really small." It drove me crazy.

Like the onion, one challenge in working with men is their unwillingness to peel away the layers. Like an onion, men are stubborn to reveal what's at their core. It often never happens, and men struggle through life unwilling to share their pain. But that's exactly what needs to happen.

Struggling men need to pull out the fears they try the hardest to hide.

Admit fear is seen as a weakness, but fear isn't a weakness. The unwillingness to respond to it is a weakness. Pulling fear out of a man is a great task. A woman who has learned the art of pulling fear out of her man is a wife most coveted. Besides sin, fear may be the final layer of a man. If you know his deepest fear, you know him better than most.

One can't discover courage without uncovering fear. What do you fear the most? Let's strip away the onion from our basic fears to those that dwell deeply, near the heart.

Sometimes we refuse to partake in activities because we're afraid of public exposure. God commanded Joshua to not only be "strong and courageous" but not be "terrified (and) discouraged." Just as courage stands with trust, fear stands with trembling. Peel away the onion. Share your fears with a trusted friend.

Then, conquer them one by one.

# LOCKING ARMS

*He appointed military officers over the people and assembled them before him in the square at the city gate and encouraged them with these words: "Be strong and courageous. Do not be afraid or discouraged because of the king of Assyria and the vast army with him, for there is a greater power with us than with him."*
~ 2 Chronicles 32:6-7

I have a few friends who inspire me. They challenge me to take more risks for Christ. They make me laugh, make me wonder, and often irritate me. Their differing opinions sharpen me.

The last thing I need in my life is men who agree with everything I say and do or are too afraid to challenge when a blind spot is detected. I need men who love me enough to call me out. It's tough to challenge a brother in sin, but we need gutsy men who will do it anyway. It takes guts to call out a friend. It takes discernment to recognize a blind spot.

To love is to challenge. Strength comes through resistance. When you lock arms with other men, sometimes they pull you in a different direction than intended. You may fight it, and they may fight you, but that's the dynamic when men lock and load.

We need men like Hezekiah. Hezekiah modeled a life of courage, the kind of courage that comes from God. He had the courage that wasn't afraid to take a step of faith. It was the kind of courage that inspired courage in others (2 Chronicles 32:5).

Men search their entire lives for other men who will inspire courage in them. Men need to lock arms with courage even though, at times, it may feel like locking horns.
Become a man that inspires courage by your example. Be a man worthy of locking arms with.

# STIR IT UP

*With a large army he will stir up his strength and courage against the king of the South.*
~ Daniel 11:25

If you've ever met a contrarian, you'll know it. They love to argue. They often tick people off. They look at life through different lenses. They live to contradict. They're contrarians.

If I say it's white, they say it's black. They know how to get under people's skin and are experts at doing it. Their opinion can spur us on (Hebrews 10:24-25), but more often, they tick us off.

The King of the North had men in his life who were mandated to "stir up his strength and courage." Isn't that interesting? From our passage today, we could gather that these men were designated to muster greater numbers of troops and train soldiers.

But what if it was something different? What if the King of the North had men assigned specifically to stir up his courage? What if he hand-selected men to keep his mind sharp and challenge his opinions?

Either way, it forces the question, "Who stirs me up? Who keeps my blade sharp?"

Stubborn pride is the Achilles heel for those men who refuse to invite others to stir them up. Men need to be stirred up, spurred on, and sharpened.

We don't need another agreeable Yes-man. We need some men with opposing views and philosophies. This is the power of the contrarian for those who desire being stirred up and spurred on. Who is stirring up courage in your life?

# THE BLIND EYE

*Slaves, obey your earthly masters with respect and fear, and with sincerity of heart, just as you would obey Christ. Obey then not only to win their favor when their eye is on you, but like slaves of Christ, doing the will of God from your heart.*
~ Ephesians 6:5-6

In high school, U.S. History was the only class I scored more than one hundred percent. My A-grade, however, was tainted, and I'm ashamed to tell you why. Our history teacher was a great athlete as a young man, but a biking accident left him wheelchair-bound and blind in his right eye.

His weekly exams happened to be the same worksheets the Advanced Placement students used the week before our tests. A devious student discovered this and procured the worksheets. Several of us strategically sat on the side of the room opposite our wheelchair-bound teacher's good eye on test day. Our teacher, blind to our cheating, could only see us by turning his head in our direction.

Who would've thought God would use my cheating days to share the passage for today?

The point is this. Most of us are under authority, whether it's a boss, a supervisor, or someone with seniority. Someone is usually watching on some level. But it's not impressive to obey when their "eye is on you."

Integrity works hard even when no one is watching. Integrity doesn't care who's in the room. It's not impressive to deceive authority or only work hard when being supervised. It's lying. It's cheating. It's wrong. How we spend our time at work matters. Your integrity is important to God.

Remember, "The eyes of the Lord range throughout the earth to strengthen those whose hearts are fully committed to him" (2 Chronicles 16:9).

# WRONG TARGET

*But you, man of God, flee from all this, and pursue righteousness, godliness, faith, love, endurance, and gentleness.*
~ 1 Timothy 6:11

With Beretta in hand, duck call in mouth, decoys bouncing on the river's edge, Dad, Darby, and I waited for our Nacimiento River blind to produce some birds. As the gray morning brightened, I saw two ducks heading in our direction.

They were big. I saw a green head. Mallards! Our guns lit up the dawn, sending both birds crashing into the river.

When my dog placed the drake in my hand, to my chagrin, the saw-toothed bill confirmed they were Green Hooded Mergansers—legal but not edible. In one shot, I'd be the laughingstock of the Redneck community. Sometimes you shoot the bull's eye on the wrong target. Sometimes we aim at the wrong things instead of what matters most.

Paul admonished Timothy to "flee from all this and pursue" what matters most. He lists six things that are essential in our pursuit of God. Each of these six falls into one of three categories: Upward, outward, and inward.

Upward essentials like "godliness, faith, and righteousness" focus on our vertical pursuit of God.

"Love" and "gentleness" are outward pursuits designed to show others the message of Jesus.

"Endurance" falls among the prestigious set of inward pursuits designed to build the inner resolve of a man's integrity. Don't aim at the wrong target. Instead, pursue the upward, outward, and inward essentials of Christ.

# TEAM MEETING TEN: BODY SHOP

> *"The body never lies."*
> ~ Martha Graham

What did you take away from last week's study and daily readings? What are you still processing? What challenged your current paradigm? What inspired you to grow as a man?

Most Americans experience the pleasures and lifestyles of ancient kings. We live in the most decadent time in history where, for most of us, our greatest physical problems have nothing to do with starvation and everything to do with over-indulgence.

What are you learning about your body as you age? Compare the decade you are in to the one you just left. What did you learn in your twenties that you didn't know in your teens? What about your thirties? Forties?
Fifties? Sixties? Seventies? Eighties? Nineties?

> *"More than two-thirds (68.8 percent) of adults are considered to be overweight. More than one-third (35.7 percent) of adults are considered to be obese. More than 1 in 20 (6.3 percent) have extreme obesity. Almost 3 in 4 men (74 percent) are considered to be overweight or obese."*
> ~ National Institute of Diabetes and Digestive and Kidney Diseases

# TEAM MEETING AT A GLANCE

- Opening Prayer, Weekly Announcements
- Personal and Victory Stories
- Each man will share his story — one man per week until all men have shared.
- After all men have shared their personal story, allow time each week for them to share victory stories.
- Weekly Study Closing Prayer
- Closing Prayer

> *"I acknowledge no man as my superior, except for his own worth, or as my inferior, except for his own dement."*
> ~ Theodore Roosevelt

**We are a steward (manager) of the body God gave us. It is the temple where the Holy Spirit dwells. 1 Corinthians 9:24-27 is appropriately titled, The Need for Self-Discipline. What wisdom about your body can you find here?**

Read the quote from Martha Graham. What is your body saying about you? What physical issues are you having due to overindulgence? What are you doing to fix it? Our bodies are dying. It's just a matter of time.

**How should we steward the body God has given us? What attitude should the follower of Jesus have about his body? What is a healthy philosophy to have about stewarding our body?**
John 14:15-17, 20:21-23, Romans 8:11, and
1 Corinthians 6:19-20

> *"Take care of your body. It's the only place you have to live."*
> ~ Jim Rohn

*Do you not know that in a race all the runners run, but only one gets the prize? Run in such a way as to get the prize. Everyone who competes in the games goes into strict training. They do it to get a crown that will not last, but we do it to get a crown that will last forever. Therefore I do not run like someone running aimlessly; I do not fight like a boxer beating the air. No, I strike a blow to my body and make it my slave so that after I have preached to others, I myself will not be disqualified for the prize.*
~ 1 Corinthians 9:24-27

**What is a hazardous philosophy to have? What is a reckless attitude towards our body? How have you treated your body with disregard?**

> *"Some people have a foolish way of not minding, or pretending not to mind, what they eat. For my part, I mind my belly very studiously and very carefully; for I look upon it, that he who does not mind his belly will hardly mind anything else."*
> ~ Samuel Johnson

*"The body too has its rights, and it will have them: they cannot be trampled on without peril. The body ought to be the soul's best friend. However, many good men have neglected to make it such: so it has become a fiend and has plagued them."*
~ Augustus William Hare and Julius Charles Hare,
Guesses at Truth, by Two Brothers, 1827

**What is a healthy perspective about your body? What's the healthy balance between following Jesus and stewarding our body well?**
2 Corinthians 4:16-18 and 1 Timothy 4:7-10

**What do the following verses teach us about the stewardship of our body? Has food mastered you? Have you become a slave to gluttony?**
1 Corinthians 6:12-13, 10:31-33, and 2 Peter 2:18-19

> *"Tis in ourselves that we are thus or thus. Our bodies are our gardens to which our wills are gardeners."*
> ~ William Shakespeare, Othello

**Just because something is legal doesn't mean it is helpful. It definitely doesn't mean it should be allowed into our bodies. How does self-control affect the whole man?**
Proverbs 16:32, 25:28, Galatians 5:22-23, and James 3:2-3

**Gluttony is the most visible sin in the church but is often ignored among spiritual leaders. What can the Pastoral Epistles teach us about spiritual leadership, discipline, and self-control?**
1 Timothy 3:1-7, 2 Timothy 3:1-5, Titus 1:5-9, and 2:1-8

The three Pastoral Epistles are books of the canonical New Testament: the First and Second Epistle to Timothy and the Epistle to Titus. They are presented as letters from the Apostle Paul to Timothy and to Titus. They're generally discussed as a group (sometimes with the addition of the Epistle to Philemon) and are given the title pastoral because they are addressed to individuals with pastoral oversight of churches and discuss Christian living, doctrine, and leadership issues.

**How can you model the healthy stewardship of your body to those within your sphere of influence?**

Break into groups of three or four.

My body desperately needs me too…

Take a moment today and pray for each other.

# STUDY NOTES

For the next five days, read the following entries from our **The Field Guide: A Bathroom Book for Men.**

We hope they challenge and encourage you to get in the great Arena for God. See you on the Arena Floor!

# THE FARMER WAY

*I know that everything God does will endure forever; nothing can be added to it and nothing taken from it. God does it so that men will revere him.*
~ Ecclesiastes 3:14

Living in the lush Willamette Valley, I've noticed a common theme among my farmer friends. They're meek, honest, and emotionally even-keeled. I asked one friend if this "farmer way" was a byproduct of some formal training or code of conduct.

He responded, "Farmers learn to trust in something much greater than themselves for their livelihood. There's no such thing as an atheist farmer." I heard a similar statement from my Vietnam veteran father-in-law, who once said, "There are no atheists in a fox hole."

Maybe this code is passed from father to son, generation to generation. Even the best farmers can do little more than prepare the ground for growth. No man can bring life. Germination is a miracle that farmers learn to trust.

Trust brings about a certain temperament if you will— the farmer's way.

Romans 1:20 says, "For since the creation of the world, God's invisible qualities—his eternal power and divine nature—have been clearly seen, being understood from what has been made, so that men are without excuse."

As much as men are fixers, there are certain things we're compelled to trust on faith. I woke up this morning. The sun came up. I breathe without thinking about it (except now that I'm thinking about it). My heart pumps blood. My neurons fire. My mind thinks.

I'm alive, and I have little say in the matter. I pity the man who doesn't believe in Someone larger than himself because "The fool says in his heart, ' There is no God'" (Psalm 14:1).

# SHARPEN YOUR FACE

*May the God who gives endurance and encouragement give you a spirit of unity among yourselves as you follow Christ Jesus, so that with one heart and mouth you may glorify the God and Father of our Lord Jesus Christ.*
~ Romans 15:5-6

Relationships are like peeling away the layers of an onion. The more layers stripped away, the deeper the relationship. The deeper our relationships run, the greater our ability to endure in our faith race.

The problem with men is their unwillingness to get beyond the superficial to the deeper layers of the soul. Locking arms in authentic, layer-peeling relationships is catalytic to one's faith. Proverbs 27:17 reveals something life-changing, "As one iron sharpens iron, so one man sharpens another."

The Hebrew word used to describe "another" or "countenance" (NKJV) is the word "pene" — the Hebrew word for face.

I laughed out loud, wondering, "Who sharpens my face?"

Who are the men that really know me? Who has traveled beyond the superficial layers? Who has my back? Who have I invited to call me out?

The list is small – no more than three or four.

Realize your relational stubbornness and fix it. Be bold enough to ask the hard questions and invite others to ask them of you. Sharpen someone's face. Let them sharpen yours.

Sharpening is a by-invitation-only privilege. The deeper layers are often too dark for just anyone. I'm not talking about holding hands around the campfire and singing Kumbaya. I'm talking about locking arms with trustworthy men who will sharpen my face.

Who's sharpening yours?

# THE SOUND MAN

*Teach the older men to be temperate, worthy of respect, self-controlled, and sound in faith, in love and in endurance.*
~ Titus 2:2

My friend Phil sat fifty yards behind me trying to coax an elk into range, while I sat frozen on my knees with the Eastern Oregon wind in my face. Heart pounding, I wondered if we'd get the herd bull to stop shredding the juniper and present a shot before sunset. He screamed as a challenge to all comers, knowing he was the biggest bull in the neighborhood but unwilling to leave his herd to prove it.

I can still hear the sounds of the bull thrashing the tree and screaming his curses. Certain sounds never leave us. One goal of this book is that you become more "sound in faith" than you were before picking it up.

Merriam-Webster defines the word "sound" as, "In good condition—solid and strong. Free from mistakes. Showing good judgment." Today's passage lists the characteristics of a "sound" man as one who is solid "in faith, in love and in endurance." His life is strong and free of mistakes.

He's a man of integrity.

His life, and the lives of those he loves, is built on a firm foundation able to withstand the storms of life (Matthew 7:24-27). Only time and circumstance can test the soundness of a man.

How he lives out faith, cares for those he loves, and his commitment to finishing strong take on many forms over time. The "sound" man lives in a way that others witness his faith, love, and his commitment to endure.

He is a pillar. He is firm. He is sound

# CROWN OF THORNS

*For riches do not endure forever, and a crown is not secure for all generations.*
~ Proverbs 27:24

Men are pursuers of trophies. Can you imagine the countless dollars spent annually on pursuing the next trophy? My childhood trophies are in the trash. The trophy car eventually gets sold. Those antlers end up hanging in the rafters. Look at the prized trophies hiding in obscure locations in your shed, soon-to-be on the front lawn, and be sold at a garage sale for small change.

But these "riches do not endure forever" and ultimately will lose significance. Notice the writer of Proverbs interchanges the word "forever" with "all generations." What crowns are you forging that will endure the generations?

The words "endure" and "secure" point to the answer. For an object to endure or remain secure, it must stand the test of time. It must be firm, remain solid. Our material crowns won't endure.

Our crown of thorns will. Someone once said, "One life to live is sure to pass. Only that done for God is sure to last."

The crown of thorns represents anything we do for the glory of God.

I'm not saying stop pursuing those things in life that bring renewal and joy. Be careful, however, to use the temporal only to energize you to accomplish eternal things.

If physical investments such as a career, sports, hobbies, or material possessions are an end in themselves and not a means to eternity, they hold no value. These things hold an eternal value to the degree that they are used to pursue spiritual crowns.

To pursue these for selfish gain or bragging rights is an exercise in futility at best and a wasted life at worst. Refuel your spirit with life's good things but be careful to keep it balanced.

# RED VINE MAN

*Therefore, since we are surrounded by such a great cloud of witnesses, let us throw off everything that hinders and the sin that so easily entangles, and let us run with perseverance the race marked out for us.*
~ Hebrews 12:1

Preparing to hike the twenty-two-mile round trip to the summit of Mt. Whitney in one day required packing light. My daypack contained a full water bladder, extra socks, flashlight, a rain shell, water pump, mid-layer, food, and (of course) toilet paper.

I told my hiking partner to pack light, so I thought he was joking when he shoved a one-gallon container of Red Vines (licorice) in his already over-loaded daypack. I'm still not sure why he packed the licorice. It came off the mountain unopened.

He struggled to make it to the summit, largely because he was packing too much stuff. I think of Jared whenever I read the advice in today's passage to "throw off everything that hinders."

Travel light.

Faith that perseveres throws off what slows it down. Fix, or deal with, any relationships that weigh you down. Life is too short to be held back. Hold material possessions loosely. God may ask you to "Sell everything and follow" (Luke 18:12). Be ready for that day if it comes.

Address any sin that "so easily entangles." Make your secret life public. "Confess your sins to each other and pray for each other so that you may be healed" (James 5:16).

When a man deals with relationships, repents of sin, and holds possessions loosely, he is free to climb unhindered. Pull out the items in your pack. What—or who—is weighing you down?

Deal with it before it's too late.

# NOW WHAT?!?

You just finished Book 1 of the Strong Men Study Series, defining the five essentials of manhood. You may be wondering, "Now what do I do?"

Thanks for asking. You have three options.
**Option Uno:** You can look for other resources for the men on your team.

Nah, we're just kidding. That's not an option.
**Option Dos:** You can move on to one of the other five books in the Strong Men Study Series until you've completed all five books, fifty of the team meetings, and 250 daily readings.

**Those books are:**

Book 1: The Trailhead: Protecting Integrity

Book 2: The Climb: Fighting Apathy

Book 3: The Summit: Pursuing God Passionately

Book 4: The Descent: Leading Courageously

Book 5: Trail's End: Finishing Strong

**Option Tres**: Visit our website (www.meninthearena.org) for other great resources to guide you to your best version of a man.

# THE BATHROOM BOOK

Men are confused about what a man is. Is he a hunter, an extreme sports guy, or religious? Is he strong, a warrior, or a fighter? Is he a great athlete, rich, or famous?

Better yet, how does a male know when he's crossed into manhood? Is it chronological age? Is it anatomical? Is it when he is legally called a man? Is it becoming financially independent?

Where does a man learn about being a man? Is it from his dad, a coach, television, Google, The Bachelor, or possibly Chuck Norris?

In the Field Guide: A Bathroom Book for Men, Jim Ramos uses his unique storytelling ability to tie masculine words in Scripture with everyday life. Day after inspiring day, the Field Guide weaves biblical themes of masculinity throughout the five essentials of manhood, "protecting integrity, fighting apathy, pursuing God passionately, leading courageously and finishing strong."

This book is a must-read for men. Place it at your bedside, in your office, man cave, or the back of your toilet. Use it as your favorite bathroom book. Read it daily. But be careful. The paper is no substitute for the real deal and will cut you! Only use it for reading!

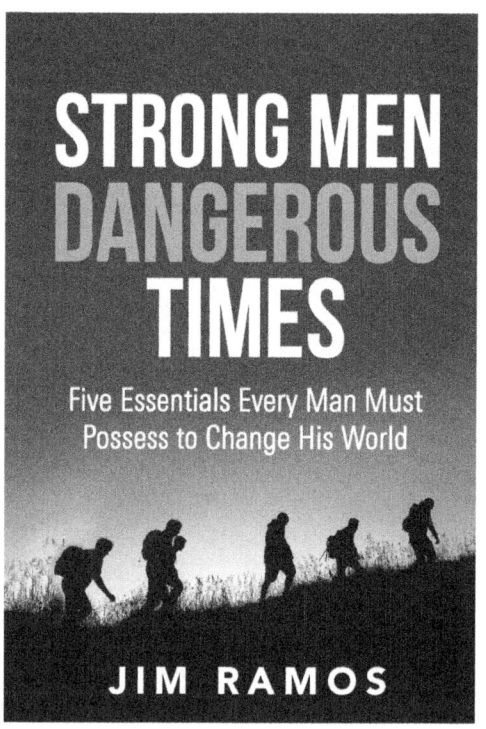

## STRONG MEN DANGEROUS TIMES

Weldon M. Hardenbrook wrote, "Let's face it. It's extremely difficult for men to act like men when so much confusion exists about the definition of manhood. For most of human history, people knew what it meant to be a man. Now, at least in modern America, no one seems to know."

But men are conquerors. They seek the next hill to die on. They long for a mission to accomplish. They need a target to shoot at, but the sights have become blurry. Men are staring aimlessly through a dense fog of cultural ambiguity, and those they love are paying the price.

In his book Strong Men Dangerous Times: Five Essentials Every Man Must Possess to Change His World, Jim Ramos answers the question men have been asking for years, "What is a man?"

The simplicity of the book is brilliantly designed for the man who's too busy to read. It's short, to the point, and loaded with life application stories and will keep you on the edge of your seat!

Order your copy today.

**ENLIST IN OUR ARMY**

### Facebook Forum
Join thousands of men from around the world in an open discussion on manhood! The Men in the Arena is a closed group for men only. It is the best free resource for men to discuss what a man is and does. Get out of the anonymous bleachers and into the Arena today!

### Weekly Equipping Blast
Visit our website and subscribe to our weekly Equipping Blast. This is not spam or advertising. It is our weekly effort to guide you towards your best version.

### Podcast
Subscribe to the Men in the Arena Podcast and learn from the top authors and experts on manhood on the planet.

# GLOSSARY

**The Definition (aka Five Essentials or Man Card):** The Men in the Arena definition of manhood is "protecting integrity, fighting apathy, pursuing God passionately, leading courageously, and finishing strong." These are the things a man does to keep his Man Card.

**Dioko:** The Greek word the Apostle Paul used in Philippians 3:12 and 14 for "press on" meaning to hunt, pursue, or chase. It's where our name for The Great Hunt for God originated before we changed it to Men in the Arena!

**Equipping Blast:** Our weekly email blast is sent to thousands of men around the world. It includes our blog, podcast links, training videos, and more! Sign up at meninthearena.org.

**Fighting Apathy:** The second of the five characteristics of manhood demanding that men fight against all cultural resistance threatening to pull them down. Failure to resist this friction over time becomes apathy or callousness. Matthew 13:13-15 defines "callousness" as a lack of feeling that results when we fail to fight against the things trying to push us down. The second book in the Strong Men Study Series: The Climb, is dedicated to this topic.

**Financial Champion:** Did you know Men in the Arena is a crowd-funded organization? Crowd-funded means we strategically partner with generous people like you to fund our ministry. Please consider joining our great team of financial champions by signing up as a monthly donor on our website.

**Finishing Strong:** This is the last of the five traits of manhood, imploring men to finish every day strong to finish life strong. Each day's strong finish compounded over time completes a strong life finish.

Finishing is not the same as finishing strong. Please refer to 2 Timothy 4:6-7. The fifth book in the Strong Men Study Series: The Trail's End is dedicated to this topic.

**Guardrails:** Imagine traveling on the narrow road Jesus spoke of in Matthew 7:13-14. Its borders are lined with guardrails meant to direct and protect you as you travel through life. Guardrails are walls or hedges a man builds around himself and those he loves. Deuteronomy 22:8 is a great reference for building guardrails.

**Intergenerational:** One of the core values of the Men in the Arena is to lock shields with men representing all generations and decades of life.

**Leading Courageously**: The fourth of five aspects of The Definition imploring a man to step up and assume the role as patriarch and spiritual leader of the household. The fourth book in the Strong Men Study Series: The Descent, is dedicated to this topic.

**Protecting Integrity**: The first and foundational component in the Man Card describing the man who is mature, complete, and unbroken. Integrity is the sum of all character traits fully formed in a man. The first book in the Strong Men Study Series: The Trailhead, is dedicated to this topic.

**Pursuing God Passionately**: The third and climactic component of the Man Card. It's our adamant belief that no man can achieve his original design without radical obedience and relentless pursuit of his Creator and King. The third book in the Strong Men Study Series: The Summit, is dedicated to this topic.

**Tag Line**: We say it all the time. "When a man gets it - everyone wins!!"

**Team Meeting**: The weekly gathering of the Men in the Arena. Team meetings are designed to be no more than one hour in length and set to meet at the same time and place each week at the discretion of the team captains.

**Vision**: Our vision is simply trusting Jesus Christ to build an army of Men in the Arena, who are becoming their best version in Christ, and changing their world (because when a man gets it - everyone wins!).

# COACHING TIPS

This Coaching Tips section is designed to help both new and seasoned Team Captains.

It offers helpful hints we've discovered in our years of running small groups with men.

Our one request is that you don't veer off course and go rogue with your team meetings. Our coaching tips are tried and true.

Feel free to add your personal style but avoid making it up as you go. We've been there—done that— and want to spare you the humiliation! Good hunting.

**Big brother is watching:** Your guys are watching you. They're watching how you live, love, serve, and run all team meetings.
Be an example.

**Bring your A-Game**: Bring your A-Game to the team meetings. Know who will and will not be present. Come prepared with notes in your workbook. If you have a co-captain, make sure you're on the same page. Men know when you come unprepared. This sends the wrong message.

**Dynamics**: How your team members are positioned in the room is crucial. The men need to sit at eye level and equidistant from the center of an eight-foot (maximum) diameter circle. If your circle, or any man, is further than four feet from center, your discussions will be greatly hindered.

**Finger on the pulse:** Your team will take on a unique identity. The morale of the men is at different levels, and group dynamics change constantly. What is the heartbeat of your men? Who's been missing? Who seems disengaged? Are you connecting with your co-captain(s)? What does your team need this week?

**Floor Stare:** Try this the next time you ask a question. Stare at the floor or at your workbook until guys begin to answer. Let them deal with the awkward silence and figure out an answer on their own.

**Half Full Glass:** Transforming lives is a journey. It's an investment into the lives of imperfect men. Even though these books are broken into ten-week bricks, our goal is to make a long-term investment in the transformational process.

But life is tough, and people are messy. When you lead your team, make sure to be positive. The negative will be easier to spot but be careful to acknowledge more positive than negative. It will pay dividends in the end.

**Preparation is Key:** Come prepared and ready to lead your team each week. The men on your team are watching you. They see the scribbled pages of preparation within the margins of The Man Card Series pages.

They also notice the blank pages when you come unprepared. Don't wing it and fling it. Bring your own thoughts and ideas to the table at every team meeting.

# NEW TEAM LAUNCH STEPS

The Launch Steps are a tool to help Captains start a successful team.

**Launch Step One: Co-Captain**
Although it is not mandatory that you do this to launch a team, we highly recommend that you have another man to lock shields with through this process. There will be times you can't make it to the group, and it's good to know that someone has your back.

Besides recruiting team members, leaders often confess that finding their co-captain was the most challenging step in launching a new team. If you already have your co-captain, great job!

If you're struggling to find a co-captain, don't be discouraged. It's normal! When you approach a potential co-captain, and he has questions about the Men in the Arena and what you're asking him to do, send him to our website (www.meninthearena.org).

There, he can join our online forum, subscribe to our Equipping Blast, and receive all the information about Men in the Arena he needs to feel confident. Now you're ready to take on Launch Step Two.

**Launch Step Two: Hit List**
Hopefully, you were able to recruit a co-captain. If so, congratulations! Now it's time to put together your team. That's what building the Hit List is all about. Did you know that Jesus recruited a larger group of disciples before he chose the Twelve? Check it out:

*"One of those days, Jesus went out to a mountainside to pray, and spent the night praying to God. When morning came, he called his disciples to him and chose twelve of them, whom he also designated apostles: Simon (whom he named Peter), his brother Andrew, James, John, Philip, Bartholomew, Matthew, Thomas, James, son of Alphaeus, Simon who was called the Zealot, Judas, son of James, and Judas Iscariot, who became a traitor."*
Luke 6:12-16

With your co-captain, create two Hit Lists of at least 10-15 potential recruits—yours and his. Commit your Hit List to prayer, asking God to direct you through the process.

Once both lists have been compiled, pray over them, and decide who will receive a formal "call" (Launch Step Three) to be on your team. Some Team Captains invite all the men on their Hit Lists, while others are more selective. This is personal preference. Some Captains struggle to recruit enough men for their team. Others have to cut their Hit List down. Team size should range from a minimum of six to fourteen members maximum.

If possible, create an intergenerational team of men ranging throughout multiple decades of life. Once the Hit List is created, move on to Launch Step Three.

**Launch Step Three: Call**
Before you call each man, make sure you have the set time, date, and place of your first meeting—the Team Launch. This is important: you and your co-captain set the meeting day, time, and place, then tell the men. Don't ask the men what they prefer.

Make a decision before inviting men to join your team. Captains that try to please everyone on this issue lose. Some men won't be able to join your team simply because of your meeting times. That's normal, and you must be okay with it.

Once verbal commitments are made, move on to Launch Step Four.

**Launch Step Four: Team List**
How Captains communicate with their teams is partly what separates the good teams from the great ones. The Team List will be used on the Buy-In (Launch Step Six) and must include: Name (and wife's name), e-mail (and wife's e-mail), and cell phone number. The sooner an e-mail and text group are created, the more effective your team will be.

Use the Team List to remind the men about your weekly meetings. This acts as a reminder and gives men a simple way to reply if they can't make it that week.

We recommend putting together a calendar of key events for your team. Include your launch day, time, and place of weekly meeting, Team Potluck (Launch Step Five), and other important dates such as birthdays, important anniversaries, and regular social gatherings.

**Launch Step Five: Team Potluck**

You're almost there! You only have a few more steps until your Team Launch! Great job! We can't overemphasize the importance of the Team Potluck, especially for the married men. Use your Team List to communicate the time, date, and location of the Team Potluck.

Give your potential team at least three weeks' notice to save the date and communicate with their wives (Who should also be included in the email). We have found that the wives are usually the ones who manage the family calendar.

You should also invite the pastor who oversees small groups at your church. Have him pray for the meal and say a few words about the value of men in God's agenda.

Your goal is 100% attendance of those invited. One Team Captain confessed that he opted out of the potluck to hurry the process, and it was a monumental mistake.

The goal of the Team Potluck is to get total buy-in from the wives and have all questions answered. If the wife is in, the man is in. Trust us! We've seen it over and over. Attendance by the wives is critical for the success of Team Potluck.

**Team Potluck Sample Agenda**
- Dinner Responsibilities
- Captains supply the drinks and dessert
- Host home supplies dinnerware
- A-M Main Dish
- N-Z Salad (or dessert)

Sample Agenda (make it better)
- Fellowship
- Food (remember to pray before eating!)
- Captain and wife introductions
- Team member and wife introductions
- Review Team Launch information (day, time, and place), commitment level (75% attendance), and other pertinent information
- Explain the Buy-In (Launch Step Six)
- Q and A
- Pray for the group

**Team Captain Commission:** We believe in partnership with the local church and highly encourage Team Captains to get commissioned by a pastor or spiritual leader. If at all possible, get commissioned during the worship service at the church you attend. If not, the potluck is an appropriate option.

Fellowship

## Launch Step Six: Buy-In

You can almost taste your Team Launch at his point. We're as excited as you to see lives transformed through your team!

All that's left is to order the books. Attrition will most likely claim some of the men, but we have found that the more the men buy in, the more committed they will be.

You can either buy the resources yourself, and the men reimburse you or send them directly to www.meninthearena.org and purchase the curriculum themselves.

## Launch Step Seven: Commission and Launch

We hinted at this in launch Step Five: Team Potluck. Did you know that in the New Testament, the Twelve Apostles, the Apostle Paul—and Jesus—were commissioned in ministry? Have you been commissioned?

If not, we highly recommend it as a model for spiritual leadership. We believe so much in the local church that we strongly urge all team captains to be commissioned by their pastor or spiritual leader. Make it a public display. Here are some elements of a commission.

- Ceremony or public worship service
- Anointing and/or laying on of hands
- Public words of affirmation
- Giving of gifts (optional)
- Witnesses
- Spiritual leader
- Predecessor
- The Holy Spirit

**Launch Step Eight: Team Launch Meeting One**

Today's the day you've been working so hard for—Congratulations! This is an informational meeting only. Do not plan on going through the curriculum. Rather, make sure all of the men have it. If you don't meet where food and drinks are served, make sure they are available. Your first meeting should be one hour long from your designated start time (start on time, end on time).

Below is a sample agenda.
- Fellowship over food and drinks (10 minutes)
- Opening Prayer
- Restate the purpose, expectations, meeting agenda. Make sure they have purchased their books. (5 minutes)
- Men share about their lives, what they expect to get from the group, and where they are in their spiritual journey (40 minutes)
- Encourage and inspire them with your personal vision for the team. Be sensitive to where each man is. Be careful not to push too hard too fast. (5 minutes)
- Closing Prayer

Thank you so much for getting out of the anonymous bleachers and into the Arena! We are pumped to partner with you on your new adventure!

# ABOUT JIM RAMOS

Thank you for taking your precious time to work through this book. I am honored and hope it inspired you on your journey towards the best you.

Lets lock arms on our journey. You can follow my journey on Facebook, Twitter, or Instagram @jimwramos.

I've been married to my best friend Shanna since 1992. She's the most important person in my life and my best friend. We love drinking coffee, traveling to tropical places, and eating out with friends.

I'm an avid book reader, enjoy fitness in the great outdoors, but my real passion is hunting. My sons are my hunting partners, along with a select few guys.

I love hanging out with men over a cup of good coffee and learning their stories. You can learn more about my story at meninthearena.org

Made in the USA
Monee, IL
24 December 2021